SUPER SIMPLE
BAKING FOR KIDS

SUPER SIMPLE BAKING FOR KIDS

**LEARN TO BAKE WITH
OVER 55 EASY RECIPES FOR
COOKIES, MUFFINS, CUPCAKES & MORE!**

CHARITY MATHEWS

Photography by Evi Abeler

ROCKRIDGE
PRESS

Interior and Cover Designer: Emma Hall
Photo Art Director/Art Manager: Karen Beard
Editor: Clara Song Lee
Production Editor: Erum Khan
Photography © 2019 Evi Abeler. Food styling by Albane Sharrard.
Author photo courtesy of Laura Wessell.

ISBN: Print 978-1-64152-319-6 | eBook 978-1-64152-320-2

FOR PHOEBE,

ESTELLE,

GEORGE,

& VIOLET,

MY FAVORITE BAKERS OF ALL.

CONTENTS

INTRODUCTION

WELCOME TO BAKING!
GET READY FOR A REAL ADVENTURE.

AS THE BAKER, YOU GET TO DECIDE EXACTLY WHAT GOES INTO EVERY RECIPE: CHUNKY PEANUT BUTTER OR SMOOTH? SPRINKLES OR CHOCOLATE CHIPS? AND YOUR CHOICES NOT ONLY AFFECT THE FLAVOR; THEY CAN ALSO CHANGE THE OUTCOME OF THE RECIPE BECAUSE EVERY TIME YOU BAKE IT'S A REAL-LIFE SCIENCE EXPERIMENT! IN THIS BOOK YOU'LL LEARN WHAT MAKES BREAD FLUFFY, HOW TO GET THE PERFECT SOFT AND CHEWY COOKIE, AND THE SURPRISING SECRET TO MOIST BANANA BREAD.

FROM COOKIES AND CAKES TO PIZZA AND PRETZELS, THERE ARE SO MANY FUN AND YUMMY TREATS HERE FOR YOU TO EXPLORE. THESE ARE MY FAVORITE RECIPES TO BAKE WITH MY KIDS AND I HOPE YOU ENJOY THEM, TOO.

LET'S GET STARTED!

CHAPTER ONE

BAKING BASICS

Baking isn't very different from making crafts. You need instructions (called a "recipe"), the right tools (measuring cups and mixing bowls, for example), and a little time. The bonus? You end up with something delicious to eat when you are done. Here are a few things you need to know before you start.

GETTING READY TO BAKE

Baking is a lot easier if you get things organized before you begin. Follow these three important steps:

1. **Read the recipe from start to finish before you begin.** Reading a recipe before you put anything in a bowl will help you avoid making mistakes. Once you've read the entire recipe, use the following handy checklist to double-check that you are ready to go.

   - Do I have enough time to make this recipe? (Check the baking time.)
   - How many servings does this recipe make? (Make sure it will serve the number of people you are hoping for.)
   - Do I have all of the ingredients? (Check the ingredients list.)
   - Do I have all of the tools needed? (Check the tools list.)

2. **Ask an adult to help you.** Make sure you have adult supervision. You may need help with some steps like grating, zesting, or chopping. An adult should also be on hand to help with the oven (opening and closing, inserting and removing pans).

BAKING VERSUS COOKING

Baking typically involves using the oven, while *cooking* happens on top of the stove. There's another key difference, too: Baking requires chemistry. Ingredients such as eggs, baking soda, and baking powder work with the heat of your oven to transform wet batter into fluffy cakes, muffins, and more. But the quantities of these ingredients need to be correct from the start, so follow the recipe carefully. Once you've put a baking pan into the oven, you generally can't make changes.

SAFETY FIRST!

Always follow these simple rules in the kitchen:

- Wash your hands with soap and water before starting a recipe.

- When chopping, grating, and zesting, curl your fingers under (like making a claw) to protect your fingertips.

- Always use pot holders when handling hot pans.

- Don't eat raw dough. (You can get sick from eating raw eggs.)

- Wash your hands after handling eggshells. (Unwashed eggs can have bacteria on the surface).

- Clean up spills right away to avoid slips and falls.

- Stay focused on your task. Most cuts and burns happen when you look away.

- Wear an apron to keep your clothes clean.

- Take your time.

- Always ask for help when you need it.

3. **Prepare your work area.** Make sure you have a clear and clean work space.

- Give yourself plenty of room to make your recipe without having to worry about knocking things over or getting them dirty.
- Wipe the counter clean.
- Lay out all of the ingredients you will need (just like on the cooking shows).
- Pull out all of your tools: measuring spoons and cups, bowls, pans, etc.
- Keep a garbage and compost bowl nearby so you don't have to run across the kitchen to throw anything away.
- Keep a damp cloth on hand for wiping your hands or the counter as you go.

EQUIPMENT

Having the right equipment makes baking more fun because it helps you get the best results. While basic baking doesn't require expensive pans and specialty tools, you will need a few key pieces to make the recipes in this book. I've listed the ones I think you need to get started.

KITCHEN TOOLS

 Baking cups Paper or silicone baking cups. These make cleanup super easy.

 Cookie scoop A cookie scoop is smaller than an ice cream scoop. Using a cookie scoop lets you drop equal portions of cookie dough onto your baking sheet, which means the cookies bake evenly.

 Electric mixer A handheld electric tool that makes it easier to mix ingredients together in a large mixing bowl.

 Ice cream scoop Not just for ice cream! This handy tool lets you scoop out equal portions of batter for cupcakes and muffins, which means they will bake evenly. Be sure to use a scoop with a thumb release to make removing the batter a snap.

 Metal sifter A woven metal screen used to remove clumps from dry ingredients like flour and baking powder.

 Metal whisk A stirring tool that helps mix air into wet ingredients.

Nonstick cooking spray Prevents baked goods from sticking to the pan.

Parchment paper A heat-resistant paper (usually up to 400°F) for covering baking pans to prevent sticking. Available in rolls or pre-cut rectangles that fit on baking sheets. A good alternative to non-stick cooking spray.

Pastry blender A hand-held cooking utensil that looks like a rounded claw with a handle. It's used to combine butter into flour.

Rubber or silicone spatula A spatula with a soft rubber or silicone blade. Great for mixing of all kinds, especially gentle ingredients. Also ideal for scraping batters out of bowls.

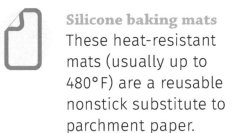

Silicone baking mats These heat-resistant mats (usually up to 480°F) are a reusable nonstick substitute to parchment paper.

Stand mixer This appliance comes with a large bowl and has different attachments, like a whisk and a paddle, to mix ingredients for you. If you already have an electric mixer, then you do not need a stand mixer.

MEASURING CUPS AND BOWLS

Dry measuring cups
Used for measuring dry ingredients such as flour and sugar. Usually comes in a set of standard measures, such as 1 cup, ½ cup, ⅓ cup, and ¼ cup. Handles make scooping easier.

Liquid measuring cups
Used for measuring wet ingredients such as milk or oil. Usually made of glass or clear plastic so you can see the measure from the side.

Mixing bowls Used to combine ingredients. Can be plastic, ceramic, or metal. You'll usually need one large and one small mixing bowl.

PANS AND RACKS

Baking sheet A flat metal pan used in the oven. Also called a "cookie sheet" or "half sheet pan." They take up almost a full rack inside most ovens.

Cooling rack A wire rack used for cooling baked goods after they come out of the oven. Helps air circulate around the item or pan so baked goods cool evenly and quickly.

Loaf pan A pan made of either glass or metal, 8½-by-4½-inches. Used to make loaves of bread or small cakes.

Muffin pan A baking pan with individual cups or wells for making muffins or cupcakes. Comes in 6- or 12-cup trays for standard size muffins and 24-cup trays for mini-muffins.

BAKER'S PANTRY

Having a well-stocked pantry means you can bake whenever you feel like it. Below are the basic ingredients I like to keep on hand.

IN THE PANTRY

All-purpose flour A general-use white flour. Store in an airtight container where it'll stay fresh for up to a year.

Baking powder Also used to help batter rise. More powerful than baking soda. Replace baking powder every few months to keep it fresh and effective.

Baking soda Also known as "sodium bicarbonate." Produces tiny bubbles in batter to help it rise. Stored in an airtight container, it will keep for up to 12 months.

Brown sugar Granulated sugar with molasses added to it. Soft and moist, but can harden if left in the air. Store in an airtight container.

Canola oil A good neutral-tasting oil. Oil helps keep baked goods moist.

Chocolate

- **Chocolate chips:** Small pieces of chocolate. The most common flavor is "semi-sweet," but you can find dark, milk, and even white chocolate in almost every grocery store.
- **Unsweetened chocolate:** Also called "baking chocolate." Used almost exclusively in baking, this is pure chocolate with no sugar added. It comes in a thick bar but don't take a bite: Without sugar, chocolate tastes very bitter.
- **Unsweetened cocoa powder:** Made from ground cacao seeds. This is another pure chocolate product that tastes very bitter on its own.

Confectioners' sugar Also known as "powdered sugar." Very finely ground granulated sugar with cornstarch added to prevent lumps. You can make your own confectioners' sugar: In a blender, combine 1 cup granulated sugar with 1 tablespoon cornstarch, and blend for about 3 minutes.

Food coloring Edible liquids or gels that add concentrated color to foods. You can find natural (made from real foods like beets) or artificial coloring. I like to use natural food coloring.

Granulated sugar Regular crystallized white sugar. Used in most baking. Store in an airtight container to prevent it from hardening.

Sprinkles Confetti-type candies used for decorating. Available in a variety of sizes and colors.

Vanilla extract Real or "pure" vanilla extract is made from vanilla beans. It has a much stronger flavor than imitation vanilla, which is made from vanillin (an extract from wood pulp). I like to use pure vanilla.

IN THE REFRIGERATOR

Butter Always use salted butter for the recipes in this book. To soften butter, set it on the counter overnight or heat it in a microwave for 10 to 15 seconds.

Eggs All of the recipes in this book call for large eggs. For best results, remove eggs from the fridge 10 to 15 minutes before using so they come to room temperature.

Heavy cream Cream that contains a higher amount of fat (35 percent), as opposed to regular cream (15 percent). Used to make whipped cream. (Whips best when kept very cold.)

KEY BAKING SKILLS

Master a few basic baking skills and you'll be able to bake anything you set your mind to! As Julia Child, a famous cook, once said, "Try new recipes, learn from your mistakes, be fearless, and above all have fun!"

GREASING THE PANS

A baker's nightmare is pulling a wonderful dish out of the oven, only to have it stick to the pan. Here's how to avoid that:

Use parchment paper or a silicone baking mat. Line a baking sheet with parchment paper or a silicone mat. Your cookies or scones will slide right off, which also makes cleanup easy.

Coat pans with nonstick cooking spray. For cake, loaf, and muffin pans, a generous coating of nonstick cooking spray will keep your baked goods from sticking.

GETTING TO ROOM TEMPERATURE

The simplest way to bring eggs and butter to room temperature is to leave them on the counter overnight. If this isn't possible, here are two quick tricks:

Warming eggs Hold the eggs in your hands for 1 to 2 minutes. The heat from your palms should bring them to room temperature.

Softening butter Place a stick of butter in a microwave-safe bowl. Heat in the microwave for 10 seconds. If you need it softer, heat for another 5 seconds but watch the middle, which will soften first and turn into a puddle if you're not careful.

MEASURING THE INGREDIENTS

Wet and dry ingredients require different tools to measure them:

Dry ingredients Use metal or plastic measuring cups to measure dry ingredients. Always spoon the item into the measuring cup, filling completely to the rim. Then, using the flat side of a knife, level off the top. The only exception is flour, because it will pack down too much and make your dough too thick. The secret to measuring flour is simple: Use a spoon to fluff up your flour before scooping it into the measuring cup.

Wet ingredients Use glass measuring cups to measure wet ingredients like water, oil, or milk. Place the measuring cup on a flat surface, then pour the liquid into the measuring cup. Bend down so your eyes are level with the markings on the side of the cup. Look at the middle of the cup, not at the sides, which will be higher. One exception: For small amounts of liquid such as vanilla, use a measuring spoon and fill it to the top.

MIXING THE DOUGH OR BATTER

There's more to mixing than you might think. You'll use different methods at different times. Here are the techniques you'll use in this book:

Mix the wet ingredients. Using a whisk, whip together ingredients like eggs, milk, or oil until well combined.

Sift the dry ingredients. A metal sifter placed over a mixing bowl is a simple way to add dry ingredients without clumping. Pour ingredients like flour and baking soda into the sifter and then carefully shake or tap it. Gently stir any remaining ingredients with a spatula to make sure everything has worked its way through the mesh.

Cream the butter. This is usually required at the beginning of a recipe. Use a stand mixer or electric mixer to whip the butter and sugar together until light and fluffy.

Cut in the butter with a pastry blender. Recipes for pie and biscuits require the careful blending of cold butter into dry flour. With a sturdy handle and 5 or 6 sharp curved blades, a pastry blender is the perfect tool for the job. Press the pastry blender into the butter and flour mixture, twisting it and working it up and down, until your dough looks like little white peas. This will give your baked dough a wonderful flaky texture and butter flavor.

Flour the surface. Sprinkle a handful of flour on a clean, flat surface before placing the dough on top. This helps prevent the dough from sticking. You can also coat a rolling pin with a little flour before rolling out dough.

Avoid overmixing. Unless you're making dough that requires kneading, stop mixing as soon as you see your ingredients come together. Overmixing can make tough cakes and pastries.

Knead the dough. To make bread dough soft, you've got to knead it. Use the heel of your hand to press down in the center of your dough. Then fold the dough in half. Repeat until you get a soft, pillowy ball. This can sometimes take up to 10 minutes, so be patient.

Fold in the ingredients. This means to gently combine a light, delicate ingredient with a heavier ingredient, keeping as much air in the mixture as possible. Use a rubber spatula to scoop down under and around the mixture until it's combined.

WORKING WITH PIE DOUGH

Working with pie dough gets easier with practice.

Roll the pie dough. Always work on a clean, flat surface. Sprinkle the work surface with a handful of flour then set your dough on top. Rub a little flour on your rolling pin and start rolling, pushing the dough away from you and rotating the dough as you go. This is how you'll get a round shape. Aim for an even dough that's ¼ inch thick (a little thinner than a chopstick).

Move the dough. When it's time to transfer your rolled dough to a pie pan, gently roll it up on the rolling pin. Move the rolling pin over the pie pan and unroll. If the dough isn't big enough, remove it, place it back on a floured surface, and keep rolling.

MEASURING OUT BATTER OR COOKIE DOUGH

To make sure your cookies, muffins, and cupcakes bake evenly, follow these tips:

Dividing the dough for cookies. When dropping your dough on a baking sheet, it's important to keep each portion the same size so your cookies bake evenly. If you have a mix of sizes on

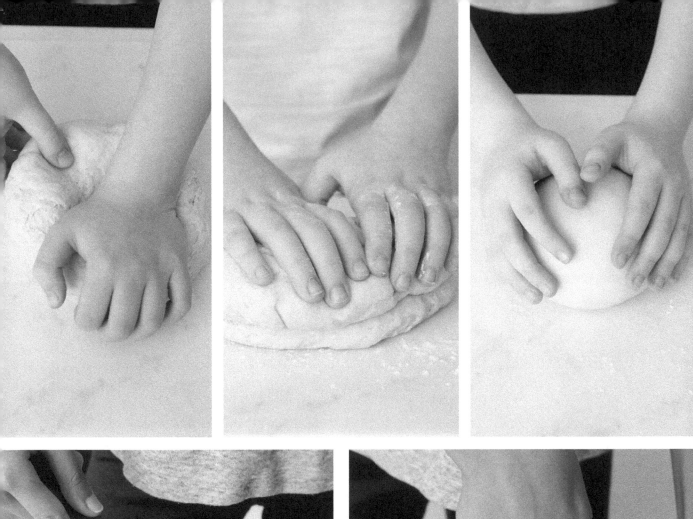

your pan, little cookies will burn before bigger ones are done. I like to use a cookie scoop (which looks like a small ice cream scoop) to measure the dough equally. Most cookies get bigger when baked so space them about 2 inches apart. Generally, you should be able to fit 12 cookies on each baking sheet.

Filling muffin pans. It's important to fill your muffin cups evenly so muffins and cupcakes cook at the same rate. An ice cream scoop with a thumb release is the perfect way to measure batter evenly with the least amount of mess.

Filling round cake pans. To get an even amount of batter into each cake pan, use a 1-cup measuring cup to dole out the batter, one scoop at a time, alternating between pans.

SEPARATING THE EGGS

Of the many ways to separate egg yolks from the whites, these are the easiest:

Hold the yolk in your hand. Crack an egg into a bowl, pick up the yolk, and let the whites fall through your fingers.

Pour the yolk back and forth. Crack an egg in half so the shell comes apart into two pieces. Working over a bowl, transfer the yolk back and forth from eggshell to eggshell until the whites fall away and you're left with only the yolk in the shell.

Use an empty water bottle. Break a whole egg into a bowl. Unscrew the cap from a clean, empty water bottle. Squeeze the bottle (to press the air out) and place the top next to the yolk in the bowl. Relax your fingers and the yolk should zoom up into the bottle.

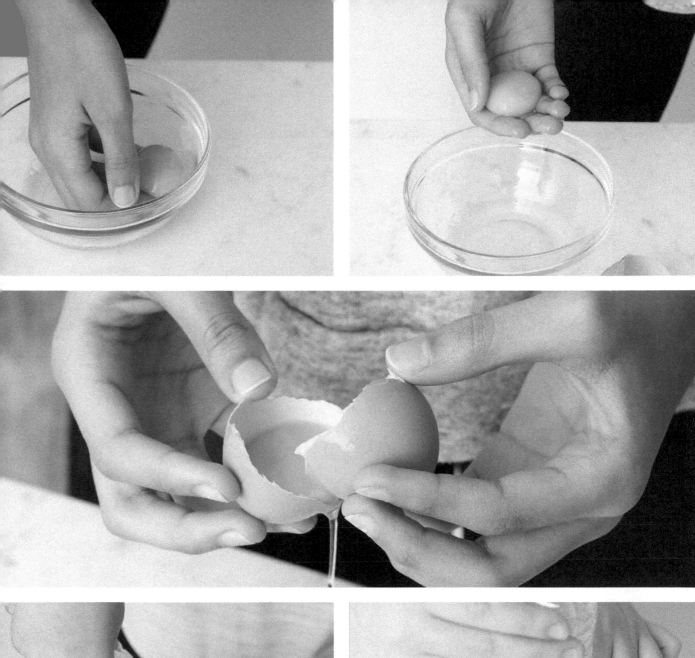

USING SHARP TOOLS

It takes time to develop the skills—and the confidence—you need to work on your own with sharp tools. Nothing is more discouraging to a new baker than getting hurt so don't be shy about asking for help.

KNIVES

Chopping and slicing are typically the first skills cooks learn. Follow these guidelines to keep your fingers safe:

- Always use a small chef's knife or plastic child-friendly knife.

- When chopping, curl the tips of your fingers under to protect them.

- Pay attention to what you are cutting. Don't get distracted.

- Use a cutting board. If the board is slipping, set it on top of a damp kitchen towel.

- When cutting, position fruit or vegetables so the flat side is down and more stable.

- Take your time. Never rush through the process of slicing or chopping.

GRATERS AND MICROPLANES

To shred or zest, use a box grater or Microplane (which is a very fine kitchen grater with many tiny sharp blades). Be careful—it's very easy to cut yourself while you're at it.

- Position the grater or Microplane over a cutting board.

- To zest citrus, wash it first, then rub the rind against the Microplane or the smallest holes on the box grater.

- To shred fruits or vegetables, use the largest holes on a box grater.

- Always stop shredding when you get close to your fingers. Ask an adult to finish up.

 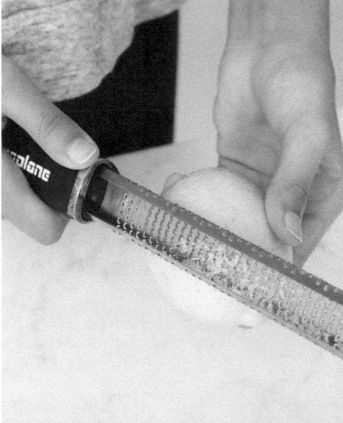

USING THE STOVE

Some recipes will require you to melt ingredients like butter or chocolate or to prepare sauces and glazes on the stove. Following these guidelines will help keep you from getting burned.

- Always ask an adult to be available before using the stove.
- Never forget when you've got a burner on.
- Keep pot handles pointed away from you.
- Pot handles might become very hot so be cautious when touching them.
- Oil can spatter so keep the heat low and never put your face close to a hot pan.
- Have a heat-safe spoon or spatula on hand before you start a recipe.
- Remember to turn off the burners when done.
- Don't set anything flammable on a burner, even if you think the burner's cooled off.

USING THE OVEN

You can't bake without an oven! Here's how it works:

Preheating. Most recipes will ask you to turn on the oven as the first step. This is so the oven can reach the right temperature by the time you're ready to put your pan in.

Baking. Generally speaking, this simply means cooking a dish in the oven, instead of on the stove with a burner.

Trapping the heat. Try not to open the oven door more often than you need to. Every time you do, heat escapes that could be used to cook your dish quickly and evenly.

Avoid banging while baking. Slamming doors can disrupt cakes and burst precious air bubbles (which is what helps them rise). To keep them from falling, handle the oven door carefully.

TIPS FOR BAKING SUCCESS

Baking is not always as forgiving as cooking. It requires careful measurements and some basic techniques, but you can do it! Follow these rules for your best chances of success:

Always read the whole recipe before you start. Many a baker has been fooled into starting a dish only to find that they're missing a key ingredient halfway through.

Follow the directions the first time you make a recipe. The first time I make any recipe, I always follow the instructions carefully. But the second time, I sometimes add a pinch of this or remove a bit of that to make it even better.

Be patient. Your first few projects may not turn out as pretty as the picture. That's okay! It takes a lot of practice to make professional-looking baked goods.

Use the right tools. If you don't have the right size pan or tool, your dish may not turn out as well as you'd like. Try another recipe for which you have everything you need.

Prep well. Always preheat the oven and generously grease your pans.

Take the time to measure. Because baking is so much about chemistry, you need to have the correct mix of ingredients for the best results.

Get it into the oven. The only time to hustle in baking is after you pour the batter into a pan. The faster you get it into a hot oven, the higher the chances your baked good will be light and fluffy.

Keep it even in the middle. Most cakes (and other baked goods) bake best on the middle rack of the oven. Rotating the pan once halfway through (turning it from front to back) will help your dish to bake evenly.

Don't be afraid to try new things (but do get recommendations). Look online for highly rated recipes or ask your friends and family for their favorites. When you know someone else likes a dish, it's worth the effort to remake it yourself.

Never apologize. If your recipe doesn't turn out the way you hoped, serve it with pride anyway. You took the time and effort to make something yourself and you deserve to enjoy the results, no matter what.

ABOUT THE RECIPES

All of the recipes in this book are suitable for bakers ages 6 to 12. To help you identify which recipes you may want to start with, we've rated the recipes by level of difficulty with one muffin, two muffins, or three muffins:

EASY Most of these recipes involve the most basic baking steps, perfect for beginners. Mix your ingredients, put them in a pan, and bake in the oven. You'll find simple recipes for everything from frosting to garlic bread and basic homemade dough.

MODERATE These recipes move on to the next skill level, including steps like rolling out pie dough, using puff pastry, or decorating with fresh fruit.

HARD These recipes involve steps that require a little more care. For example, you might fill cupcakes with jam or cover a layer cake with frosting. Some of these recipes have steps like boiling dough (for homemade pretzels!) and cooking vegetables on the stove (for veggie calzones!)

Each recipe includes a list of ingredients *and* a list of the kitchen tools you'll need, as well as step-by-step instructions. Some recipes may require the help of an adult—these recipes have an "Ask an Adult" tip.

If you can't eat nuts, look for recipes with the "nut-free" label. In some instances you may be able to substitute your favorite no-nut butter.

At the end of each recipe, you'll find tips to help you avoid mistakes or make the dish more easily.

RAINBOW MERINGUES, PAGE 29

CHAPTER TWO

COOKIES, BARS, AND BITE-SIZE TREATS

From classic chocolate chip cookies to rainbow meringues and sprinkle-studded whoopie pies, this chapter contains 13 gorgeous treats everyone will love. Most recipes are simple enough for beginner bakers, but look for the "Ask an Adult" tips on a few steps, such as adding food coloring, slicing bars, or heating a saucepan. Let's go!

RECIPES

TIPS AND TECHNIQUES

Size and spacing When dropping your cookie dough on a baking sheet, it's important to keep each portion the same size so your cookies bake evenly. If you have a mix of sizes on your pan, little cookies will burn before bigger ones are ready. I like to use a cookie scoop (which looks like a small ice cream scoop) to measure the dough equally.

Most cookies get bigger when baked so space them about 2 inches apart. Generally, you should be able to fit 12 cookies on each baking sheet.

Pans and prepping We use three kinds of pans in this chapter:

- baking sheet
- 8-by-8-inch square pan
- 24-cup mini-muffin pan

We also prepare the pans in two different ways so our desserts don't stick:

- lining with parchment paper
- coating with nonstick cooking spray

Baking sheets You'll use baking sheets to make all of the cookies. Line baking sheets with a big piece of parchment paper or a silicone baking mat and nothing will stick.

Mini-muffin pans To make miniature treats you'll need a mini-muffin pan. Just give it a good coating with nonstick cooking spray and you'll be ready.

Square baking pans To make bars, you'll need a square pan. Most are either 8 or 9 inches and made of glass or metal. A nice coating of nonstick cooking spray will keep your treats from sticking, but most bars will be easier to remove from the pan if you line them with a sheet of parchment paper that reaches all the way over the edges. After your dessert is baked (and cooled for a few minutes), grab the sides of the paper and lift up. Place on a cutting board and cut into bars or squares, as needed.

WHEN IS IT DONE?

You'll know your item is ready to come out of the oven when:

1. **The tops are puffy.**
2. **The edges are golden.**
   Don't worry if the tops deflate a bit as they cool. That's normal.

For one sheet of cookies, you'll want to bake them in the center rack of the oven. If you are baking two sheets of cookies at a time, use the top and bottom racks of the oven, be sure to arrange the racks before you heat the oven, and remember to swap and rotate the pans halfway through for even cooking.

STORING

How long do cookies keep? Most cookies will be delicious for 3 to 4 days if you keep them in an airtight container.

Baking later. Some cookies bake better with cold dough. If the recipe requires it, cover the bowl with plastic or foil and refrigerate for at least 1 hour. Or shape the dough into a ball, wrap in plastic, and refrigerate for up to 1 week.

Freezing dough. Form your dough into a log shape. Wrap in plastic wrap, then pop the log inside a zip-top bag. Write the name of your dough with the date and it'll be good in the freezer for up to 2 months. To bake from frozen, thaw dough in the refrigerator overnight before using.

RAINBOW MERINGUES

Meringues are made from whipping egg whites with sugar. They are crisp on the outside and moist and fluffy like marshmallows on the inside. The only thing that makes these even better is the rainbow coloring.

	NUT-FREE	MAKES 24 MERINGUES	PREP TIME 15 MINUTES	BAKE TIME 1 HOUR 15 MINUTES

TOOLS/EQUIPMENT

Baking sheet

Parchment paper or silicone baking mat

Stand mixer fitted with whisk attachment or mixing bowl and electric mixer

Measuring cups and spoons

Rubber spatula

Large mixing bowl

2 small bowls

Ice cream scoop with thumb release

Empty water bottle (optional)

INGREDIENTS

4 egg whites, at room temperature (see Ask an Adult)

¼ teaspoon cream of tartar

1 cup granulated sugar

Food coloring of your choice (2 different colors)

1. Preheat the oven to 300°F.
Line the baking sheet with parchment paper or a silicone mat.

2. Whip the egg whites.
In the mixing bowl, beat the egg whites and cream of tartar on low speed just until combined. While mixing, gradually add the sugar until combined. Increase the mixer speed to medium and continue whipping until the egg whites look glossy and form stiff peaks (this means the mixture will stand up straight when you lift the mixer), about 5 minutes.

3. Color the meringue.
Using a rubber spatula, divide the meringue into three equal portions: Leave one portion in the mixing bowl, and divide the other two portions between two separate smaller bowls. Add a drop or two of food coloring to each of the small bowls. Gently stir each until the color looks well blended. >>

TIP Cream of Tartar is the secret weapon when it comes to making meringues. It helps whipped egg whites become fluffier and more stable.

ASK AN ADULT to help you separate the eggs. An easy way to separate the egg yolks from the egg whites is by using an empty water bottle like a vacuum: Break 4 eggs into a small bowl, being careful not to break the yolk. Take the lid off an empty water bottle. Place the neck near a yolk and squeeze the middle of the bottle. Then loosen your grip. The yolk will shoot up into the bottle. (You can use the egg yolks in another dish or freeze them in an ice-cube tray for later.)

4. **Create rainbow swirls.**
Using a rubber spatula, carefully add both of the colored mixtures back into the same bowl with the white mixture, placing them side by side. Then, still using the spatula, draw two circles inside the mixing bowl, cutting through all the colors to make swirls. Using an ice cream scoop, drop the swirled mixture onto the parchment-lined baking sheet, spacing about 2 inches apart.

5. **Bake the meringues.**
Place the baking sheet in the preheated oven and bake the meringues for 25 minutes. Turn the oven off (do not remove the pan) and let the meringues cool in the oven for another 50 minutes. Meringues will keep in an airtight container at room temperature for up to 4 days.

THUMBPRINT JAM COOKIES

These cookies look like tiny volcanos erupting with jam (or any other sweet filling you fancy).

 NUT-FREE | MAKES 22 COOKIES | PREP TIME 20 MINUTES | BAKE TIME 15 MINUTES

TOOLS/EQUIPMENT

Stand mixer fitted with
  paddle attachment
  or mixing bowl and
  electric mixer
Measuring cups and spoons
Rubber spatula
Parchment paper or silicone
  baking mats
2 baking sheets
Spatula
Wire racks
Small spoon

INGREDIENTS

1 cup (2 sticks) salted butter,
  very soft
¾ cup granulated sugar
1 large egg
1 teaspoon vanilla extract
2½ cups all-purpose flour
¼ teaspoon baking soda
½ cup jam (raspberry,
  strawberry, or apricot)

1. **Cream the butter and sugar.**
In the mixing bowl, combine the butter and sugar. Beat on medium speed until light and fluffy, about 2 minutes, stopping to scrape down the sides of the mixing bowl with a rubber spatula if needed.

2. **Add the wet ingredients.**
Add the egg and vanilla. Beat again until combined, about 1 minute.

3. **Add the dry ingredients.**
Add the flour and baking soda. Mix on low speed until the flour is completely incorporated, about 30 seconds.

4. **Chill the dough.**
Using your hands, shape the dough into a disc. Cover tightly in plastic wrap. Refrigerate for at least 1 hour or overnight.

5. **Preheat the oven to 350°F.**
Line the baking sheets with parchment paper or silicone mats. >>

ASK AN ADULT to help you rotate the pans in the hot oven.

6. **Shape the cookies.**
Using the palms of your hands, roll a spoonful of the dough into a 1-inch ball. Place on the prepared baking sheets. Repeat with the remaining dough, spacing each about 2 inches apart. Using your thumb, make a round indent in the top of each ball by pressing 2 or 3 times.

7. **Bake.**
Transfer the pans to the preheated oven. Bake the cookies for 10 to 15 minutes, until they are golden. Switch the position of the pans halfway through (move the top pan to the bottom, and vice versa; also rotate the pans back to front).

8. **Let cool.**
Remove the pans from the oven. Let the cookies cool on the baking sheets for 3 to 5 minutes. Using a spatula, transfer the cookies to the wire racks to cool completely.

9. **Fill cookies.**
Using a small spoon, fill each thumbprint with jam. Cookies will keep in an airtight container at room temperature for up to 3 days.

SUGAR COOKIES

These cookies are soft and sweet and go great with a warm cup of cocoa. Serve them plain or frosted (see pages 117, 118, and 119 for yummy frosting recipes).

 NUT-FREE | MAKES 24 COOKIES | PREP TIME 40 MINUTES | BAKE TIME 12 MINUTES

TOOLS/EQUIPMENT

Stand mixer fitted with paddle attachment or mixing bowl and electric mixer
Measuring cups and spoons
Rubber spatula
2 baking sheets
Parchment paper or silicone baking mats
Spatula
Wire racks

INGREDIENTS

1 cup salted butter, very soft
1 cup granulated sugar
1 teaspoon vanilla extract
2 large eggs
2¼ cups all-purpose flour
½ teaspoon baking powder
½ teaspoon baking soda
½ teaspoon salt

1. **Cream the butter and sugar.**
In the mixing bowl, combine the butter and sugar. Beat on medium speed until light and fluffy, about 2 minutes, stopping to scrape down the sides of the mixing bowl with a rubber spatula if needed.

2. **Add the wet ingredients.**
Add the vanilla and eggs. Beat again for 1 minute. Scrape down the sides of the bowl again.

3. **Add the dry ingredients.**
Add the flour, baking powder, baking soda, and salt. Mix just until combined, about 20 seconds.

4. **Chill the dough.**
Cover the bowl of dough with plastic wrap. Place in the refrigerator for 1 hour or overnight.

5. **Preheat the oven to 350°F.**
Line the baking sheets with parchment paper or silicone mats.

6. **Shape the cookies.**
Remove the dough from the fridge. Pinch off a golf ball–size chunk of dough. Using the palms of your hands, form the dough into a 2-inch ball. Place the balls on the parchment-lined baking sheets. Repeat with the remaining dough, spacing the balls about 2 inches apart.

7. **Bake.**
Place the pans in the oven and bake for 10 to 12 minutes, until golden at the edges. Switch the position of the pans halfway through (move the top pan to the bottom, and vice versa; also rotate the pans back to front).

8. **Let cool.**
Remove the pans from the oven. Let the cookies cool on the pans for 3 to 5 minutes. Using a spatula, transfer the cookies to the wire racks to cool completely. Cookies will keep in an airtight container at room temperature for up to 1 week.

PEANUT BUTTER COOKIES

It only takes four ingredients to make the best peanut butter cookies you'll ever dunk in a glass of milk. Plus, since they're made without flour, they're gluten-free.

	MAKES	PREP TIME	BAKE TIME
	16 COOKIES	5 MINUTES	12 MINUTES

TOOLS/EQUIPMENT
Baking sheet
Parchment paper or silicone baking mat
Large mixing bowl
Wooden spoon
Measuring cups and spoons
Cookie scoop or large spoon
Fork
Wire rack
Spatula

INGREDIENTS
1 cup smooth peanut butter
1 cup granulated sugar
1 large egg
1 teaspoon vanilla extract

TIP If you like a little crunch, use chunky peanut butter or add ½ cup of chopped salted peanuts in step 2. For a peanut-free version, substitute an equal amount of no-nut butter.

1. **Preheat the oven to 350°F.**
   Line the baking sheet with parchment paper or a silicone mat.

2. **Make the dough.**
   In the large mixing bowl using a wooden spoon, combine the peanut butter, sugar, egg, and vanilla. Stir until well combined.

3. **Prepare the cookies.**
   Scoop up a heaping tablespoon of dough. Roll the dough into 2-inch balls with your hands. Place on the prepared baking sheet, spacing 2 inches apart. Using a fork, press down on each cookie twice, in a crisscross pattern.

4. **Bake.**
   Bake for 10 to 12 minutes, until golden around the edges.

5. **Let cool.**
   Remove the pan from the oven. Let the cookies cool on the pan for 3 to 5 minutes. Using a spatula, transfer the cookies to the wire rack to cool completely. Cookies will keep in an airtight container at room temperature for up to 1 week.

STRAWBERRY-OATMEAL BREAKFAST BARS

These breakfast bars are packed with goodness but taste just like dessert!
Make them on the weekend to enjoy all week long.

 NUT-FREE | MAKES 16 BARS | PREP TIME 5 MINUTES | BAKE TIME 35 MINUTES

TOOLS/EQUIPMENT
9-by-13-inch baking pan
Parchment paper
Large mixing bowl
Measuring cups and spoons
Serrated knife

INGREDIENTS
1 cup (2 sticks) salted butter,
  very soft
1½ cups old-fashioned oats
1½ cups whole-wheat flour
½ cup lightly packed
  brown sugar
½ cup ground flaxseed or
  wheat germ
1 teaspoon baking soda
½ teaspoon salt
¾ cup low-sugar strawberry
  jam or fruit spread
⅓ cup dried sweetened fruit,
  such as cranberries

1. **Preheat the oven to 375°F.**
   Line the baking pan with enough parchment paper so the edges reach over the sides of the pan. (You'll pull up on the paper to remove the bars from the pan when they're done baking.)

2. **Make the oat base.**
   In the large mixing bowl, combine the butter, oats, flour, brown sugar, flaxseed (or wheat germ), baking soda, and salt. Use clean hands to make sure all the ingredients are well mixed. Squeeze the oat mixture until it forms a big ball.

3. **Bake the oat base.**
   Set aside 1 cup of the oat mixture. Using the palms of your hands, evenly press the rest evenly into the parchment-lined baking pan. Place the pan in the **preheated oven.** Bake for 10 minutes.

4. **Add the jam layer.**
   Remove the pan from the oven (keep the oven on) and let the base cool for about 10 minutes. When cool, spread a thick layer of jam over the top. Sprinkle it evenly with the dried fruit.

5. **Add the topping.**
   Crumble the reserved oat mixture on top. (You should see jam peeking through.)

6. **Bake.**
   Return the pan to the hot oven. Bake for 25 minutes, until golden on the edges.

7. **Let cool.**
   Remove the pan from the oven. Let the breakfast bars cool in the pan for 5 to 10 minutes. Holding the edges of the parchment, transfer it to a cutting board. Using a serrated knife, cut into 16 bars. These bars will keep in an airtight container in the refrigerator for up to 1 week.

CHOCOLATE GRANOLA BARS

Customize your own granola bars with this recipe! From raisins and peanuts to dried cranberries or M&M's, there's no limit to the flavors you can create. Add up to 1 cup of additional mix-ins when you mix the dry ingredients together.

 MAKES 8 BARS | PREP TIME 15 MINUTES | BAKE TIME 20 MINUTES

TOOLS/EQUIPMENT
8-by-8-inch baking pan
Parchment paper
Large mixing bowl
Rubber spatula
Measuring cups and spoons
Small saucepan
Sharp knife

INGREDIENTS
2 cups old-fashioned oats
1 cup sweetened
   flaked coconut
½ cup ground flaxseed or
   wheat germ
1 cup walnut pieces
1 cup chocolate chips
2 tablespoons salted butter
½ cup honey
½ teaspoon salt
1 teaspoon vanilla extract

1. **Preheat the oven to 300°F.**
Line the baking pan with enough parchment paper so the edges reach over the sides of the pan. (You'll pull up on the paper to remove the bars from the pan when they're done baking.)

2. **Mix the dry ingredients.**
In the mixing bowl, use a rubber spatula to combine the oats, coconut, flaxseed (or wheat germ), and walnuts. Stir well.

3. **Melt the chocolate.**
In a small saucepan over medium heat, combine the chocolate chips, butter, honey, salt, and vanilla. Stir continuously, about 1 minute, until the chocolate has melted.

4. **Mix the wet and dry ingredients.**
Pour the melted chocolate mixture over the oat mixture. With a rubber spatula, stir until all the oats are coated. (Use your hands if you like, but ask an adult first to make sure the chocolate isn't too hot!) >>

TIP Really press the oat mixture into the pan! The more you pack it down, the better your granola bars will hold together. To keep the mixture from sticking to your hands, grease your hands with a little bit of butter.

ASK AN ADULT to help you cut the granola into bars.

5. **Press the oat mixture into the pan.**
Transfer the oat mixture to the prepared pan and, using your hands, spread it out so it's flat and even.

6. **Bake.**
Place the pan in the preheated oven. Bake the mixture for 20 minutes, until the edges are just golden.

7. **Let cool.**
Remove the pan from the oven. Let the granola cool in the refrigerator for 20 minutes.

8. **Cut the bars.**
Using your hands, press down on the granola one more time to ensure it is packed tightly. Holding the edges of the parchment paper, transfer it to a cutting board. Using a sharp knife, cut into 8 rectangles. Granola bars will keep in an airtight container at room temperature for up to 1 week.

SOFT AND CHEWY CHOCOLATE CHIP COOKIES

Who doesn't like chocolate chip cookies? This recipe is perfect as is, but if you'd like a little crunch, mix in 1 cup of chopped walnuts along with the chocolate chips at the end of step 5.

 NUT-FREE | MAKES 18 TO 20 COOKIES | PREP TIME 10 MINUTES | BAKE TIME 10 MINUTES

TOOLS/EQUIPMENT

2 baking sheets

Parchment paper, silicone baking mats, or nonstick cooking spray

Stand mixer fitted with paddle attachment or mixing bowl and electric mixer

Rubber spatula

Measuring spoons and cups

Cookie scoop or large spoon

Spatula

Wire rack

INGREDIENTS

½ cup (1 stick) salted butter, very soft

¾ cup lightly packed brown sugar

1 large egg

1 teaspoon vanilla extract

1¾ cups all-purpose flour

½ teaspoon baking soda

¼ teaspoon salt

¾ cup chocolate chips

1. **Preheat the oven to 350°F.**
   Line the baking sheets with parchment paper or silicone mats, or spray with non-stick cooking spray.

2. **Cream the butter and sugar.**
   In the mixing bowl, combine the butter and brown sugar. Beat on medium speed until light and fluffy, about 2 minutes, stopping to scrape down the sides of the mixing bowl with a rubber spatula if needed.

3. **Add the wet ingredients.**
   Add the egg and vanilla. Beat again for 1 minute, until the ingredients are well incorporated.

4. **Add the dry ingredients.**
   Add the flour, baking soda, and salt. Mix on low speed until the ingredients are well combined, about 30 seconds.

5. **Add the chocolate chips.**
   Pour the chocolate chips into the bowl. Using your hands, mix them evenly throughout the dough. >>

TIP Why use your hands to mix? Dough that's been mixed too much becomes tough. Mixing with your hands instead of an electric mixer makes a softer cookie.

TIP Make them match! Make sure your cookies are all the same size so they bake evenly.

ASK AN ADULT to help you rotate the pans in the hot oven.

6. **Shape the cookies.**
Scoop up a heaping tablespoon of dough. Using the palms of your hands, roll into a 2-inch ball. Place on the baking sheet. Repeat with the remaining dough, spacing evenly, about 2 inches apart. You should be able to fit 12 dough balls on a baking sheet.

7. **Bake.**
Place the pans in the preheated oven. Bake for 8 to 10 minutes, until slightly brown on the edges. Switch the position of the pans halfway through (move the top pan to the bottom, and vice versa; also rotate the pans back to front).

8. **Let cool.**
Remove the pans from the oven. Let the cookies cool on the pans for 3 to 5 minutes. Using a spatula, transfer the cookies to the wire rack to cool completely. Cookies will keep in an airtight container at room temperature for up to 1 week.

SNICKERDOODLE BARS

Have you ever heard of snickerdoodles? Nope, they aren't puppies. They're cinnamon-dusted cookie bars! You'll love their buttery sweet taste.

 NUT-FREE | MAKES 12 TO 16 BARS | PREP TIME 10 MINUTES | BAKE TIME 30 MINUTES

TOOLS/EQUIPMENT

8-by-8-inch baking pan
Parchment paper
Stand mixer fitted with paddle attachment or mixing bowl and electric mixer
Measuring cups and spoons
Rubber spatula
Small bowl
Serrated knife

FOR THE BARS

½ cup (1 stick) salted butter, very soft
1 cup granulated sugar
1 large egg
2 teaspoons vanilla extract
1 cup all-purpose flour

FOR THE TOPPING

2 tablespoons granulated sugar
1 tablespoon ground cinnamon

1. **Preheat the oven to 350°F.**
   Line the baking pan with enough parchment paper so the edges reach over the sides of the pan. (You'll pull up on the paper to remove the bars from the pan when they're done baking.)

2. **Mix the sugar and wet ingredients.**
   In the mixing bowl, cream together the butter and sugar until light and fluffy, about 2 minutes, stopping to scrape down the sides of the bowl with a rubber spatula if needed. Add the egg and mix until combined, about 30 seconds. Scrape the sides of the bowl again and add the vanilla. Mix for another 30 seconds.

3. **Add the flour.**
   Add the flour and mix on low speed until the flour is completely incorporated into the mixture.

4. **Prepare the base.**
   Scrape the dough into the parchment-lined pan. Using your fingers, press the dough evenly into the bottom of the pan.

5. **Add the topping.**
In a small bowl, stir together the sugar and cinnamon. Using your fingers, sprinkle the mixture evenly over the top of the base.

6. **Bake.**
Place the pan in the preheated oven and bake for 30 minutes, until the dough is set, the edges are lightly browned, and the cinnamon sugar has cracked.

7. **Let cool.**
Remove the pan from the oven. Let the snickerdoodles cool in the pan for 5 to 10 minutes.

8. **Cut into squares.**
Once cool, remove the bars from the pan by pulling up on the parchment paper. Transfer to a cutting board. Using a serrated knife, cut into squares. These bars will keep in an airtight container at room temperature for up to 1 week.

RAINBOW SPRINKLES WHOOPIE PIES

What do you call two soft rainbow sprinkles cookies held together by a thick layer of colorful frosting? A party for your mouth!

 NUT-FREE | MAKES 11 WHOOPIE PIES | PREP TIME 20 MINUTES | BAKE TIME 10 MINUTES

TOOLS/EQUIPMENT

Stand mixer fitted with paddle attachment or mixing bowl and electric mixer
Measuring cups and spoons
Rubber spatula
2 baking sheets
Parchment paper or silicone baking mats
Cookie scoop or large spoon
Spatula
Wire racks
3 small bowls

FOR THE COOKIES

1 cup (2 sticks) salted butter, very soft
1 cup granulated sugar
2 large eggs
2 teaspoons vanilla extract
½ teaspoon almond extract
3 cups all-purpose flour
1½ teaspoons cornstarch
1 teaspoon baking powder
1 teaspoon baking soda
¾ cup candy sprinkles

1. **Cream the butter and sugar.**
   In the mixing bowl, combine the butter and sugar. Beat on medium speed until light and fluffy, about 2 minutes, stopping to scrape down the sides of the mixing bowl with a rubber spatula if needed.

2. **Add the wet ingredients.**
   Add the eggs and the vanilla and almond extracts. Beat again until combined, about 1 minute.

3. **Add the dry ingredients.**
   Add the flour, cornstarch, baking powder, and baking soda. Mix on low speed until the flour is completely incorporated, about 30 seconds. Using your hands, mix the sprinkles into the dough.

4. **Chill the dough.**
   Cover the bowl of dough with plastic wrap and refrigerate for at least 20 minutes.

5. **Preheat the oven to 350°F.**
   Line the baking sheets with parchment paper or silicone mats. >>

FOR THE FROSTING

½ cup (1 stick) salted butter, very soft

8 ounces (1 stick) cream cheese, at room temperature

½ cup confectioners' sugar

1 teaspoon vanilla extract

Food coloring (your choice of 3 colors)

ASK AN ADULT to help you rotate the pans in the hot oven.

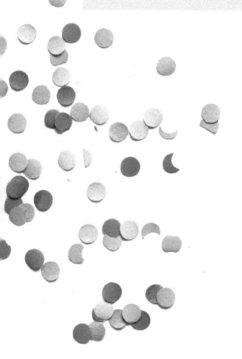

6. **Shape the cookies.**
Using a cookie scoop or large spoon, measure out 2 tablespoons of dough. Using the palms of your hands, roll the dough into a ball and place on the prepared baking sheet. Repeat with the remaining dough to make 22 total balls, spacing each ball about 2 inches apart.

7. **Bake.**
Place the pans in the preheated oven. Bake the cookies for 8 to 10 minutes, until they look fluffy. Switch the position of the pans halfway through (move the top pan to the bottom, and vice versa; also rotate the pans back to front).

8. **Let cool.**
Remove the pans from the oven. Let the cookies cool on the baking sheets for 3 to 5 minutes. Using a spatula, transfer the cookies to the wire racks to cool completely.

TIP Running short on time? Skip the sandwich step and enjoy these cookies without the frosting!

TIP Don't try to add the frosting until your cookies have cooled completely. Otherwise you'll have a melty mess!

9. **Make the frosting.**

In a clean mixing bowl, whisk together the butter, cream cheese, confectioners' sugar, and vanilla. Divide the frosting into three bowls. Add 1 to 2 drops of your choice of food coloring to each bowl. Stir well.

10. **Assemble whoopie pies.**

Spread the flat bottom of a cooled cookie with about 2 tablespoons of frosting. Cover with a second cookie to make a sandwich. Repeat with remaining cookies. Whoopie pies will keep in an airtight container at room temperature for up to 1 week in the refrigerator.

LEMON BARS

These squares have a crispy shortbread crust and a wonderfully tart lemon filling. With both lemon zest and lemon juice, this classic treat just might make you pucker up.

 NUT-FREE | MAKES 16 BARS | PREP TIME 10 MINUTES | BAKE TIME 45 MINUTES

TOOLS/EQUIPMENT

8-by-8-inch baking pan

Parchment paper

Stand mixer fitted with paddle attachment or mixing bowl and electric mixer

Measuring cups and spoons

Zester or Microplane

Rubber spatula

Sharp knife

FOR THE CRUST

12 tablespoons (1½ sticks) cold salted butter, cut into small pieces

1½ cups all-purpose flour

6 tablespoons granulated sugar

FOR THE FILLING

1¼ cups granulated sugar

¼ cup all-purpose flour

4 large eggs

2 tablespoons freshly grated lemon zest (about 2 lemons)

¾ cup fresh lemon juice (about 4 lemons)

¼ cup confectioners' sugar

1. **Preheat the oven to 350°F.**
   Line the baking pan with parchment paper so the edges reach over the sides of the pan. (You'll pull up on the paper to remove the bars from the pan after baking.)

2. **Make the crust.**
   In the mixing bowl, combine the butter, flour, and sugar on medium speed until the mixture looks like large grains of sand, about 1 minute. Transfer the butter mixture to the parchment-lined pan. Using your hands, press down until the mixture is firm and even. Bake in the preheated oven for 22 to 25 minutes or just until the edges start to turn golden brown.

3. **Make the filling.**
   While the crust is baking, combine the sugar, flour, eggs, and lemon zest and juice in a large bowl. Whisk until smooth. Set aside while the crust finishes baking. >>

TIP Using a metal sifter will help you evenly dust the bars with sugar. Simply pour the confectioners' sugar into the sifter and tap the sifter with your fingers. Just be mindful not to put the confectioners' sugar on too early. It'll dissolve into the lemon bars after a few minutes.

ASK AN ADULT to help you zest the lemons and cut the lemon bars into squares.

4. **Bake.**
When the crust is ready, remove the pan from the oven. Give the lemon mixture a quick stir, and then carefully pour it onto the warm crust. Return the pan to the oven and bake for about 20 minutes more, until the top looks firm (be careful not to let the edges burn).

5. **Let cool.**
Remove the pan from the oven and let cool for at least 1 hour. Then transfer to the refrigerator to cool completely. (Never stick a hot pan directly into the fridge.)

6. **Serve.**
Holding the edges of the parchment, transfer to a cutting board. Using a sharp knife, cut into 16 squares. Just before serving, dust with the confectioners' sugar. Lemon bars will keep in an airtight container in the refrigerator for up to 5 days.

MINI STRAWBERRY SHORTCAKES

Tiny shortcakes filled with whipped cream and fresh strawberries are a match made in heaven. Want to change up the filling? Vanilla pudding, chocolate-hazelnut spread, or your favorite frosting are all yummy alternatives.

 NUT-FREE | MAKES 20 COOKIES | PREP TIME 10 MINUTES | BAKE TIME 10 MINUTES

TOOLS/EQUIPMENT
Mini-muffin pan
Nonstick cooking spray
Stand mixer fitted with
    paddle attachment
    or mixing bowl and
    electric mixer
Measuring cups and spoons
Rubber spatula
Teaspoon
Fork
Wooden spoon

FOR THE SHORTCAKES
6 tablespoons salted butter,
    very soft
½ cup granulated sugar
1 large egg
¼ teaspoon almond extract
1 teaspoon vanilla extract
1¼ cups flour
½ teaspoon baking powder

1. **Preheat the oven to 350°F.**
Coat the mini-muffin pan with nonstick cooking spray.

2. **Cream the butter and sugar.**
In the mixing bowl, combine the butter and sugar. Beat on medium speed until light and fluffy, about 2 minutes, stopping to scrape down the sides of the mixing bowl with a rubber spatula if needed. Add the egg, almond extract, and vanilla. Mix well.

3. **Add the dry ingredients.**
Add the flour and baking powder. Mix again until the ingredients are well incorporated and the mixture forms a soft dough.

4. **Form the shortcakes.**
Using a teaspoon, scoop up 1 teaspoon of dough. Roll it into a ball between the palms of your hands. Place the ball into one of the muffin pan cups. Repeat with the remaining dough. Using your thumb, press down on the center of each ball to form a little cup. Using the tines of a fork, prick the bottom of each cup to prevent it from puffing up when baked. Bake the cups for 10 minutes. >>

FOR THE FILLING

½ cup heavy cream

2 ounces cream cheese, at room temperature

½ cup confectioners' sugar

1 teaspoon vanilla extract

2 cups diced hulled strawberries

TIP You can make these treats up to 1 day in advance. Store the baked shortcakes and the filling in separate containers, and assemble the dessert just before serving.

TIP For an even easier dessert, simply fill the shortcakes with store-bought whipped cream and top with fresh strawberries.

5. **Make the filling.**
In a clean mixing bowl, whisk together the cream, cream cheese, confectioners' sugar, and vanilla until smooth. Cover and refrigerate until ready to use.

6. **Let cool.**
Remove the pan from the oven and, using the handle of a wooden spoon, press down the centers (they puff up during baking). Allow the shortcakes to cool completely in the pan, about 20 minutes.

7. **Fill the cups.**
Remove the shortcakes from the pan. Using a small spoon, fill each to the brim with the cream mixture. Top with the diced strawberries. Serve immediately.

CANDY BAR BLONDIES

Blondies are the sweeter cousins to brownies, and in this recipe, they are also the perfect base to use for—and share—leftover holiday candy.

	MAKES	PREP TIME	BAKE TIME
	12 TO 16 BARS	15 MINUTES	27 MINUTES

TOOLS/EQUIPMENT

9-by-13-inch baking pan
Parchment paper
Large mixing bowl
Wooden spoon
Measuring cups and spoons
Rubber spatula
Serrated knife

INGREDIENTS

12 tablespoons (1½ sticks) salted butter, very soft
1 cup lightly packed brown sugar
2 large eggs
2 teaspoons vanilla extract
2 cups all-purpose flour
½ teaspoon baking soda
1½ cups chopped chocolate bars (cut into small pieces)

1. **Preheat the oven to 325°F.**
   Line the baking pan with enough parchment paper so the edges reach over the sides of the pan. (You'll pull up on the paper to remove the bars from the pan when they're done baking.)

2. **Mix the sugar and wet ingredients.**
   In the mixing bowl, stir together the butter, brown sugar, eggs, and vanilla until well combined.

3. **Add the dry ingredients.**
   Add the flour and baking soda. Stir until well combined. Add the chocolate pieces and stir just until evenly incorporated.

4. **Transfer the dough to the pan.**
   Scrape the cookie dough into the pan, using a rubber spatula to spread it evenly. >>

ASK AN ADULT to help you cut the blondies into squares.

5. **Bake.**
Transfer the pan to the preheated oven. Bake for 24 to 27 minutes, until the edges become lightly browned.

6. **Let cool.**
Remove the pan from the oven. Let the blondies cool in the pan for 5 to 10 minutes. Holding the edges of the parchment, transfer the blondies to a cutting board. Using a serrated knife, cut into 12 to 16 squares. These blondies will keep in an airtight container at room temperature for up to 1 week.

DOUBLE BERRY CREAM PUFFS

You won't believe how easy it is to transform this handful of simple ingredients into a fancy dessert.

 NUT-FREE | MAKES 24 PUFFS | PREP TIME 10 MINUTES | BAKE TIME 25 MINUTES

TOOLS/EQUIPMENT

Baking sheet

Parchment paper or silicone baking mat

Wooden spoon

Stand mixer fitted with whisk attachment or mixing bowl and electric mixer

Measuring cups

Teaspoon

INGREDIENTS

24 puff pastry cups

1 cup heavy cream

¼ cup strawberry, blackberry, or raspberry jam

1 cup fresh raspberries, blackberries, or blueberries for decoration

TIP Very cold cream whips best so keep it in the fridge until you're ready to use it!

1. **Preheat the oven to 400°F.**
Line the baking sheet with parchment paper or a silicone mat.

2. **Bake the cups.**
Arrange the puff pastry cups on the prepared baking sheet, spacing them about 2 inches apart. Bake in the preheated oven for 20 to 25 minutes, until completely puffed up and golden brown.

3. **Let cool.**
Remove the pan from the oven. Using the handle of a wooden spoon, press down on the center of each puff pastry cup until it's flat. Let cool completely on the pan. >>

TIP Can't find puff pastry cups at the store? Cut regular puff pastry sheets into 2-inch squares and then press each square into a mini-muffin pan. Bake for 10 minutes, until puffed up and golden brown. Follow the instructions for flattening the centers in step 3.

4. **Whip the cream.**
In the mixing bowl, combine the cream and jam. Whip until the mixture forms stiff peaks.

5. **Fill the cups.**
Using the teaspoon, fill each pastry cup with the cream mixture.

6. **Top with berries.**
Decorate each puff with a berry or two. Serve immediately.

BANANA BREAD, PAGE 86

CHAPTER THREE

MUFFINS AND QUICK BREADS

Quick breads use baking powder or baking soda instead of yeast to help them rise, which means they can be made—you guessed it—quickly! You'll love all of the muffins, sweetened breads, and scones in this chapter. Once you get the hang of these recipes, you can switch up some of the ingredients to make them your own. From strawberries to cinnamon to chocolate, think of all the possibilities . . .

RECIPES

TIPS AND TECHNIQUES

Preparing baking pans. For the recipes in this chapter, you'll need either a regular-size 12-cup muffin pan, a baking sheet (sometimes called a cookie sheet), or a standard loaf pan (8½-by-4½ inch). To prevent the batter from sticking, coat the pans with nonstick cooking spray. Be sure to get all the corners so the muffins or bread will come out easily. Use paper or silicone baking cups when instructed. For scones, use a baking sheet lined with parchment paper or a silicone baking mat.

Measuring batter for muffins. It's important to fill your muffin cups evenly so the muffins cook at the same rate. When you don't have enough batter to fill the whole pan, fill the empty muffin cups with water. This also helps your muffins cook evenly.

Combining wet and dry ingredients.
All of these recipes use a combination of wet and dry ingredients. If you mix them together all at once, the batter might not rise and your baked goods will turn out hard or flat. My favorite technique for mixing them is also the easiest: Whisk the wet ingredients in a big mixing bowl first (things like eggs, oil, or butter). Then set a sifter over the top of your mixing bowl. Add the dry ingredients (flour, baking soda, sugar) and sift (see page 12). Use a rubber spatula to gently mix everything together until you don't see streaks of flour—then stop! In just one bowl, you'll have everything you need for soft muffins, quick bread, and scones every time.

WHEN IS IT DONE?

When finished baking, muffins and bread should spring back when you press down lightly on the tops with your finger. Scones should be firm to the touch and golden on the edges. You can also insert a toothpick into the center; if it comes out clean (no batter or crumbs sticking on), take the pan out of the oven.

STORING

Scones are best eaten on the same day they are made, but muffins and breads will keep for 3 to 5 days. Store them in an airtight container on the counter. Plus, baked muffins and bread freeze beautifully! Store them in freezer-safe bags for up to 2 months. Just thaw them out on the counter when you are ready to enjoy them.

LEMON-POPPYSEED MUFFINS

The outside of a lemon peel is called the "zest," and it contains tons of flavor. Using both the lemon zest and the juice gives baked goods a punch of citrus flavor.

 NUT-FREE | MAKES 12 MUFFINS | PREP TIME 5 MINUTES | BAKE TIME 20 MINUTES

TOOLS/EQUIPMENT
12-cup muffin pan
Nonstick cooking spray
Large mixing bowl
Whisk
Measuring cups and spoons
Sifter
Rubber spatula
Ice cream scoop with
  thumb release
Zester or Microplane
Wire rack

FOR THE MUFFINS
1½ cups plain yogurt
2 tablespoons fresh lemon
  juice (about 1 lemon)
1½ tablespoons freshly grated
  lemon zest (about 2 lemons)
2 large eggs
½ cup (1 stick) salted butter,
  very soft
3 cups all-purpose flour
1 cup granulated sugar
1 tablespoon baking powder
½ teaspoon baking soda
1 tablespoon poppy seeds

1. **Preheat the oven to 375°F.**
Line the muffin pan with paper baking cups or coat with nonstick cooking spray.

2. **Mix the wet ingredients.**
In the mixing bowl, whisk together the yogurt, lemon juice, lemon zest, eggs, and butter until everything is well incorporated.

3. **Add the dry ingredients.**
Set a sifter over the mixing bowl. Pour the flour, sugar, baking powder, and baking soda into the sifter and shake. Use a spatula to gently stir until all of the dry ingredients are in the bowl. Add the poppy seeds. Using a spatula, gently mix the batter just until the flour has been incorporated.

FOR THE GLAZE

¼ cup confectioners' sugar
¼ cup fresh lemon juice
   (about 2 lemons)

ASK AN ADULT to help zest the lemons using a Microplane or the smallest holes on a box grater. Once your lemons are zested, cut them in half and squeeze the juice out. Hold the lemons over a strainer to trap any seeds.

4. **Bake.**

Using an ice cream scoop, fill each muffin cup three-quarters full. Transfer the pan to the preheated oven. Bake the muffins for 18 to 20 minutes, until the tops of the muffins spring back when lightly touched or a toothpick inserted into the center comes out clean.

5. **Let cool.**

Remove the pan from the oven. Let the muffins cool in the pan for about 5 minutes, then transfer the muffins to a wire rack to cool completely.

6. **Glaze.**

In the small bowl, whisk together the confectioners' sugar and lemon juice. Using a spoon, drizzle the glaze on top of the muffins. These muffins will keep in an airtight container at room temperature for up to 3 days.

BLUEBERRY MUFFINS

You can make these muffins using either fresh or frozen blueberries. If you use frozen blueberries, coat them with 2 tablespoons of flour to soak up the extra water before mixing them into the batter. You can skip the sugar topping if you like, but it adds a wonderful texture and sweet flavor.

	NUT-FREE	MAKES 10 MUFFINS	PREP TIME 10 MINUTES	BAKE TIME 18 MINUTES

TOOLS/EQUIPMENT

12-cup muffin pan
Baking cups (paper or silicone) or nonstick cooking spray
Large bowl
Whisk
Measuring cups and spoons
Sifter
Rubber spatula
Ice cream scoop with thumb release
Wire rack

INGREDIENTS

½ cup milk
⅓ cup canola oil
1 large egg
1 teaspoon vanilla extract
1½ cups all-purpose flour
¾ cup granulated sugar
2 teaspoons baking powder
½ teaspoon salt
1 cup fresh or frozen blueberries
2 tablespoons raw sugar, for dusting on top

1. **Preheat the oven to 400°F.**
   Line the muffin pan with paper baking cups or coat with nonstick cooking spray.

2. **Mix the wet ingredients.**
   In the mixing bowl, whisk together the milk, oil, egg, and vanilla.

3. **Add the dry ingredients.**
   Set a sifter over the mixing bowl. Add the flour, sugar, baking powder, and salt. Shake the sifter until all the lumps have been removed and the ingredients are in the bowl. Using a spatula, gently mix just until the flour is incorporated.

4. **Add the blueberries.**
   Very gently, fold the blueberries into the batter.

TIP Fill the empty cups in the muffin pan with water to help the muffins bake evenly.

5. **Bake.**

Using the ice cream scoop, divide the batter evenly between 10 cups. Sprinkle the tops with the raw sugar. Bake the muffins for 15 to 18 minutes, until the tops spring back when lightly touched or a toothpick inserted into the center comes out clean.

6. **Let cool.**

Remove the pan from the oven. Let the muffins cool in the pan for about 5 minutes, then transfer the muffins to a wire rack to cool completely. These muffins will keep in an airtight container in the refrigerator for up to 5 days.

STRAWBERRY MUFFINS

These muffins are filled with the taste of summer. Fresh berries are always nice, but you can use frozen berries, too. Just toss them in 2 tablespoons of flour to soak up the icy juices before adding them to the batter in step 4.

 NUT-FREE | MAKES 12 MUFFINS | PREP TIME 15 MINUTES | BAKE TIME 20 MINUTES

TOOLS/EQUIPMENT

12-cup muffin pan
Nonstick cooking spray
Large bowl
Whisk
Measuring cups and spoons
Sifter
Rubber spatula
Ice cream scoop with thumb release
Wire rack

INGREDIENTS

2 large eggs
1 cup (2 sticks) salted butter, very soft
1 cup granulated sugar
1¼ cups milk
1 teaspoon vanilla extract
3 cups all-purpose flour
1 tablespoon baking powder
½ teaspoon baking soda
2 tablespoons ground cinnamon
2 cups diced hulled strawberries

1. **Preheat the oven to 375°F.**
Line the muffin pan with paper baking cups or coat with nonstick cooking spray.

2. **Mix the sugar and wet ingredients.**
In the mixing bowl, whisk the eggs until frothy. Add the butter, sugar, milk, and vanilla. Whisk until smooth.

3. **Add the dry ingredients.**
Set a sifter over the mixing bowl. Add the flour, baking powder, baking soda, and cinnamon to the sifter and shake. Use a rubber spatula to gently stir until all of the dry ingredients are in the bowl.

4. **Add the berries.**
Gently fold in the diced strawberries using a rubber spatula, just until combined. >>

TIP You can switch up the fruit! Frozen mango or pineapple (tossed in 2 tablespoons of flour) would be delicious.

5. **Bake.**

Using an ice cream scoop, fill each muffin cup three-quarters full. Transfer the pan to the preheated oven. Bake the muffins for 18 to 20 minutes, until the tops of the muffins spring back when lightly touched or a toothpick inserted into the center comes out clean.

6. **Let cool.**

Remove the pan from the oven. Let the muffins cool in the pan for about 5 minutes, then transfer them to a wire rack to cool completely. These muffins will keep in an airtight container in the refrigerator for up to 5 days.

PUMPKIN SPICE MUFFINS

These pumpkin spice muffins are sure to become your favorite fall treat. My family loves them. And because they freeze so well, this recipe makes two dozen, so you can share them or eat them throughout the autumn season.

	NUT-FREE	MAKES 24 MUFFINS	PREP TIME 10 MINUTES	BAKE TIME 25 MINUTES

TOOLS/EQUIPMENT

2 (12-cup) muffin pans
Nonstick cooking spray
Large mixing bowl
Whisk
Measuring cups and spoons
Sifter
Rubber spatula
Ice cream scoop with
    thumb release
Wire rack

INGREDIENTS

1 (15 ounce) can pure
    pumpkin purée
    (not pumpkin pie filling)
4 large eggs
½ cup unsweetened
    applesauce
½ cup canola oil
1 cup granulated sugar
3 cups all-purpose flour
1 teaspoon salt
2 teaspoons baking soda
3 tablespoons pumpkin
    pie spice

1. **Preheat the oven to 350°F.**
   Line the muffin pan with paper baking cups or coat with nonstick cooking spray.

2. **Mix the wet ingredients.**
   In the bowl, whisk together the pumpkin, eggs, applesauce, and oil.

3. **Add the dry ingredients.**
   Set a sifter over the mixing bowl. Pour the sugar, flour, salt, baking soda, and pumpkin pie spice into the sifter and shake it. Use a rubber spatula to help work the mixture into the bowl. Then stir just until the mixture is combined, about 8 times. ＞＞

TIP Individual applesauce containers measure ½ cup. Save time on washing up by using the empty container to measure out the oil.

ASK AN ADULT to help you rotate the pans in the hot oven.

4. **Bake.**

Using an ice cream scoop, fill the muffin cups about three-quarters full. Bake the muffins for 20 to 25 minutes, until the tops of the muffins spring back when lightly touched or a toothpick inserted into the center comes out clean. Remember to switch the position of the pans halfway through (move the left pan to the right, and vice versa; also rotate the pans back to front).

5. **Let cool.**

Remove the pan from the oven. Let the muffins cool in the pan for about 5 minutes, then transfer the muffins to a wire rack to cool completely. These muffins will keep in an airtight container in the refrigerator for up to 1 week.

CHOCOLATE CHIP MUFFINS

To make these muffins even heartier (and prettier), dust them with a sprinkle of sweetened coconut flakes and top them with a few blueberries before you put the pan in the oven.

 | NUT-FREE | MAKES 12 MUFFINS | PREP TIME 10 MINUTES | BAKE TIME 15 MINUTES

TOOLS/EQUIPMENT

12-cup muffin pan

Baking cups (paper or silicone) or nonstick cooking spray

Large mixing bowl

Whisk

Measuring cups and spoons

Sifter

Rubber spatula

Ice cream scoop with thumb release

Wire rack

INGREDIENTS

1 cup milk

½ cup vegetable oil

2 large eggs

1½ teaspoons vanilla extract

2 cups all-purpose flour

½ cup granulated sugar

1 tablespoon baking powder

½ teaspoon salt

½ cup chocolate chips

1. **Preheat the oven to 425°F.**
Line the muffin pan with baking cups or coat with nonstick cooking spray.

2. **Mix the wet ingredients.**
In the mixing bowl, whisk together the milk, oil, eggs, and vanilla until frothy.

3. **Add the dry ingredients.**
Set a sifter over the top of your mixing bowl. Add the flour, sugar, baking powder, and salt. Shake the sifter until all the lumps have been removed and the ingredients are in the bowl. Using a spatula, gently mix just until combined. (Don't worry about a few lumps! The key to yummy muffins is not to overmix the batter.)

4. **Add the chocolate.**
Gently stir the chocolate chips into the batter. >>

TIP Use an ice cream scoop with a thumb release to measure your batter. You'll get the perfect amount every time, and make less mess, too.

5. **Bake.**

Using an ice cream scoop, fill each muffin cup three-quarters full. Transfer the pan to the preheated oven. Bake the muffins for 13 to 15 minutes, until the tops of the muffins spring back when lightly touched or a toothpick inserted into the center comes out clean.

6. **Let cool.**

Remove the pan from the oven. Let the muffins cool in the pan for about 5 minutes, then transfer the muffins to a wire rack to cool completely. These muffins will keep in an airtight container at room temperature for up to 5 days.

MIX-AND-MATCH OATMEAL MUFFINS

These muffins taste just like a nice warm bowl of oatmeal on a cold day. Best of all, you can mix in any other flavorings you like: chocolate chips, coconut, nuts, dried fruit, and more. The results are delicious every time.

	MAKES	PREP TIME	BAKE TIME
	12 MUFFINS	10 MINUTES	30 MINUTES

TOOLS/EQUIPMENT

12-cup muffin pan
Nonstick cooking spray
Large mixing bowl
Measuring cups and spoons
Whisk
Rubber spatula
Ice cream scoop with
   thumb release
Wire rack

FOR THE MUFFINS

2 large eggs
1½ cups milk
½ cup unsweetened
   applesauce
¼ cup smooth peanut butter
   or no-nut butter
3 tablespoons brown sugar
1 teaspoon vanilla extract
3 cups old-fashioned oats
1 teaspoon baking powder
1 teaspoon ground cinnamon
½ teaspoon salt

1. **Preheat the oven to 350°F.**
   Line the muffin pan with paper baking cups or coat with nonstick cooking spray.

2. **Mix the sugar and wet ingredients.**
   In the bowl, whisk together the eggs, milk, applesauce, peanut butter, brown sugar, and vanilla until smooth.

3. **Add the dry ingredients.**
   Add the oats, baking powder, cinnamon, and salt. Using the spatula, stir until combined.

4. **Add your mix-ins.**
   Using the spatula, gently fold in the nuts, seeds, fruit, or other mix-ins of your choice.

FOR THE MIX-INS

½ cup chopped nuts, sweetened flaked coconut, sunflower seeds, or chocolate chips

½ cup dried cranberries, pineapple, cherries, or raisins

TIP These muffins will keep in an airtight bag in the freezer for up to 1 month. Take one out of the freezer in the morning and it'll be thawed in time for your snack at school.

TIP For your healthiest smile, try to find dried fruit without extra sugar added.

5. **Bake.**

Using an ice cream scoop, fill each muffin cup about three-quarters full. Bake the muffins for 25 to 30 minutes, until the tops of the muffins spring back when lightly touched or a toothpick inserted into the center comes out clean.

6. **Let cool.**

Remove the pan from the oven. Let the muffins cool in the pan for about 5 minutes, then transfer the muffins to a wire rack to cool completely. These muffins will keep in an airtight container in the refrigerator for up to 1 week.

ORANGE-RASPBERRY SCONES

Scones are small biscuit-like cakes. Famously served with tea in England, kings and queens have been enjoying their sweet, buttery flavor for centuries. With this recipe, now you can, too!

 | NUT-FREE | MAKES 8 SCONES | PREP TIME 25 MINUTES | BAKE TIME 18 MINUTES

TOOLS/EQUIPMENT

Baking sheet

Parchment paper or silicone baking mat

Large mixing bowl

Measuring cups and spoons

Rubber spatula

Pastry blender or 2 butter knives

Pastry brush

Wire rack

INGREDIENTS

2 cups all-purpose flour

½ cup granulated sugar

1 tablespoon baking powder

½ cup (1 stick) salted butter, cut into small cubes

1 teaspoon freshly grated orange zest

½ cup heavy cream, plus 2 tablespoons for brushing

1 large egg

1 cup raspberries (fresh or frozen)

1. **Preheat the oven to 400°F.**
Line the baking sheet with parchment paper or a silicone mat.

2. **Mix the dry ingredients.**
In the large mixing bowl, stir together the flour, sugar, and baking powder.

3. **Add the butter and orange zest to the mixing bowl.**
Using the pastry blender, 2 butter knives, or your fingers, work the butter and zest into the flour until the mixture resembles small peas.

4. **Add the wet ingredients.**
To the flour mixture, add ½ cup of the cream and the egg. Using a rubber spatula or your hands, mix until the mixture comes together to form a dough. >>

TIP These scones taste best on the day they're made.

5. **Add the raspberries.**
Sprinkle a handful of flour on a cutting board. Dump the dough on top. Using the palms of your hands, flatten the dough into a square about ⅓ inch thick. Sprinkle the raspberries over two-thirds of the dough. Fold the last third of the dough over the berries in the middle. Gently press down on the dough, then fold it over one more time, covering the last third of the berries, so you end up with a long log.

6. **Shape the scones.**
Cut the log in half crosswise (the short way), making two squares. Cut each square into four triangles. You should end up with eight pieces.

7. **Chill the dough.**
Transfer the wedges of dough onto the prepared baking sheet. Freeze for 15 minutes.

8. **Bake.**

Remove the pan from the freezer. Put 2 tablespoons of cream in a small bowl. Using a pastry brush, brush cream over the top of each scone. Bake in the pre-heated oven for 18 minutes, until the scones are golden brown and a toothpick inserted into the center comes out clean (with no crumbs).

9. **Let cool.**

Remove the pan from the oven. Let the scones cool on the pan for about 5 minutes, then transfer the scones to a wire rack to cool completely. Enjoy warm or at room temperature. Scones will keep in an airtight container in the refrigerator for up to 3 days.

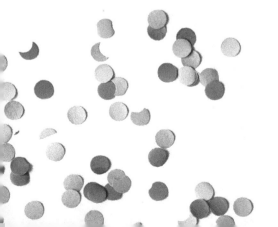

BROWN SUGAR-PECAN SCONES

If you like pancakes with maple syrup, you'll love these rich and buttery scones. Also, you can substitute any kind of nuts you like!

	MAKES	PREP TIME	BAKE TIME
	8 SCONES	15 MINUTES	15 MINUTES

TOOLS/EQUIPMENT

Baking sheet

Parchment paper or silicone
  baking mat

Large mixing bowl

Measuring cups and spoons

Pastry blender or
  2 butter knives

Rubber spatula

Pastry brush

Wire rack

INGREDIENTS

2 cups all-purpose flour

⅓ cup brown sugar

1 tablespoon baking powder

½ cup (1 stick) cold salted
  butter, cut into 8 cubes

1 cup heavy cream, plus
  2 tablespoons for brushing

½ cup chopped pecans

3 teaspoons raw sugar

1. **Preheat the oven to 450°F.**
   Line the baking sheet with parchment paper or a silicone baking mat.

2. **Prepare the dough.**
   In the mixing bowl, combine the flour, brown sugar, baking powder, and butter. Using the pastry blender, 2 butter knives, or your fingers, work the butter into the flour until the mixture resembles small peas.

3. **Add the cream.**
   Using the rubber spatula, stir in 1 cup of the cream just until combined, about 10 times.

4. **Add the pecans.**
   Using the spatula, scrape the dough onto the prepared baking sheet. Flatten the dough slightly with your hands, and sprinkle the pecans over top. Using the heel of your hand, knead the dough: press down, fold it over, press down, fold it over. Repeat 6 times until the nuts are well distributed.

ASK AN ADULT to help cut the dough into 8 pieces, like a pizza.

5. **Chill the dough.**
Shape the dough into a round about 1 inch thick. Using a knife, cut the dough into 8 even wedges, like a pizza. Transfer the scones to the prepared baking sheet, spacing them about 2 inches apart. Place the pan in the freezer for about 15 minutes.

6. **Bake.**
Remove the scones from the freezer. Place the remaining 2 tablespoons of cream in a small bowl. Using a pastry brush, brush the top of each scone with the cream. Sprinkle each with raw sugar. Put the pan in the preheated oven and bake for 13 to 15 minutes, until golden.

7. **Let cool.**
Remove the pan from the oven. Let the scones cool on the pan for about 5 minutes, then transfer them to a wire rack to cool completely. These scones will keep in an airtight container in the refrigerator for up to 3 days.

BANANA BREAD

There's a secret ingredient in this recipe: mayonnaise! It helps make this quick bread deliciously moist. It may sound strange but, trust me, you'll love the result.

 MAKES 1 LOAF   PREP TIME 10 MINUTES   BAKE TIME 1 HOUR

TOOLS/EQUIPMENT
Loaf pan
Nonstick cooking spray
Large mixing bowl
Measuring cups and spoons
Potato masher or fork
Whisk
Sifter
Rubber spatula

INGREDIENTS
3 medium bananas, mashed
½ cup mayonnaise
1 large egg
1½ cups all-purpose flour
1 teaspoon baking soda
½ teaspoon salt
¾ cup lightly packed brown sugar
½ cup chopped walnuts

1. **Preheat the oven to 350°F.**
   Coat the pan with nonstick cooking spray.

2. **Mix the wet ingredients.**
   In the mixing bowl, mash the bananas with a potato masher or fork. Add the mayonnaise and egg. Whisk together until well combined, about 30 seconds.

3. **Add the dry ingredients.**
   Place a sifter on top of the mixing bowl. Add the flour, baking soda, salt, and brown sugar, and shake into the bowl to remove any clumps. Use a spatula to gently stir together all the ingredients just until combined (stir about 8 times).

4. **Add the walnuts.**
   Gently stir in the walnuts just until combined (stir about 6 times).

5. **Bake.**
Pour the batter into the prepared pan. Bake in the preheated oven for 1 hour, rotating the pan after 30 minutes. It's ready when you can stick a toothpick in the center and it comes out clean.

6. **Let cool.**
Remove the pan from the oven. Let the bread cool completely in the pan before slicing and serving. Banana bread will keep in an airtight container in the refrigerator for up to 5 days.

CINNAMON-APPLE OAT BREAD

Full of hearty oats and sweet apples, this quick bread is perfect for breakfast and a wonderful addition to school lunchboxes—#braggingrights!

 NUT-FREE　　MAKES 1 LOAF　　PREP TIME 15 MINUTES　　BAKE TIME 55 MINUTES

TOOLS/EQUIPMENT
Loaf pan
Nonstick cooking spray
Large mixing bowl
Measuring cups and spoons
Whisk
Sifter
Rubber spatula

INGREDIENTS
2 large eggs
1 teaspoon vanilla extract
½ cup unsweetened applesauce
1 cup granulated sugar
1¼ cups all-purpose flour
1 teaspoon baking soda
1 teaspoon salt
3 teaspoons pumpkin pie spice
1 cup old-fashioned oats
2 cups cored, peeled, and chopped apples (about 2 apples)

1. **Preheat the oven to 350°F.**
Coat the pan with nonstick cooking spray.

2. **Mix the wet ingredients.**
In the mixing bowl, whisk together the eggs, vanilla, and applesauce until frothy.

3. **Add the dry ingredients.**
Set a sifter over the top of your mixing bowl. Add the flour, sugar, baking soda, salt, and pumpkin pie spice and gently shake into the bowl. Using a spatula, gently mix just until combined, about 5 times. Add the oats and apples, and then mix again, about 5 times.

4. **Bake.**
Scrape the batter into the prepared loaf pan. Place the pan in the oven and bake the bread for 55 minutes, or until a toothpick inserted in the center comes out clean.

ASK AN ADULT to help
you peel, core, and chop
the apples.

5. **Let cool.**

Remove the pan from the oven. Let the bread cool completely in the pan before slicing and serving. This bread will keep in an airtight container in the refrigerator for up to 5 days.

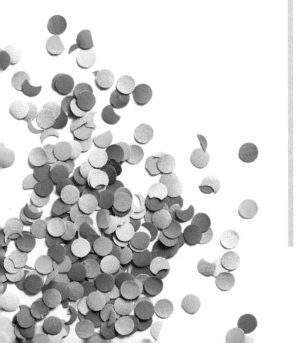

CHOCOLATE ZUCCHINI BREAD

Who would've thought zucchini would go with chocolate? You can't really taste it but that zucchini has an important job: keeping the bread moist. Plus, this recipe makes two loaves of delicious chocolate bread. One for you and one to share. (Or freeze for later. We'll never tell!)

 NUT-FREE | MAKES 2 LOAVES | PREP TIME 15 MINUTES | BAKE TIME 55 MINUTES

TOOLS/EQUIPMENT

2 loaf pans
Nonstick cooking spray
Box grater
Measuring cups and spoons
Large mixing bowl
Sifter
Rubber spatula

INGREDIENTS

1 medium zucchini, unpeeled
1 cup granulated sugar
1 cup canola oil
3 large eggs
3 teaspoons vanilla extract
1½ cups all-purpose flour
½ cup unsweetened
   cocoa powder
2 teaspoons ground
   cinnamon
1 teaspoon salt
1 teaspoon baking soda
½ teaspoon baking powder

1. **Preheat the oven to 350°F.**
Coat the loaf pans with nonstick cooking spray.

2. **Grate the zucchini.**
Shred the zucchini on the biggest setting of a box grater. You should end up with 2 cups of shredded zucchini. Set it aside.

3. **Mix the sugar and wet ingredients.**
In the mixing bowl, whisk together the sugar, oil, eggs, and vanilla until frothy.

4. **Add the dry ingredients.**
Set a sifter over the mixing bowl. Pour the flour, cocoa, cinnamon, salt, baking soda, and baking powder into the sifter and shake. Use a spatula to gently stir the dry ingredients until all of the mixture is in the bowl. Add the shredded zucchini and stir with the spatula just until combined, about 8 times.

TIP Want to take this up a notch? Make Double Chocolate Zucchini Bread! Add 1 cup of chocolate chips to the batter in step 4.

ASK AN ADULT to grate the zucchini using the large holes on a box grater. No need to peel the zucchini first! The skin is soft and edible. The adult can also help you rotate the pans in the hot oven.

5. **Bake.**
Divide the batter evenly between the two prepared pans. Put the pans in the oven and bake for 50 to 55 minutes, until a toothpick inserted in the center comes out clean. Remember to switch the position of the pans halfway through (move the left pan to the right, and vice versa; also rotate the pans back to front).

6. **Let cool.**
Remove the pans from the oven. Let the breads cool completely in the pans before slicing and serving. This bread will keep in an airtight container in the refrigerator for up to 5 days.

FRUITY CEREAL CUPCAKES, PAGE 112

CHAPTER FOUR

CAKES, CUPCAKES, AND FROSTING

Nothing says "Let's celebrate!" like cake and cupcakes. Ask an adult to prepare the pans so the cakes don't stick, and to rotate or pull hot pans out of the oven.

RECIPES

TIPS AND TECHNIQUES

Buttering pans. Cakes love sticking to the pan and when they do, your whole creation can be ruined. Your best bet for easy removal is buttering *and* flouring your cake pans. Not even the stickiest batter can get through that.

Measuring butter. Look closely at a stick of butter in its wrapper: the lines measure tablespoons. Plus, you'll see that 1 stick of butter always equals ½ cup.

Cooling cakes. Before you decorate cakes, it's important to let them cool in the pan for at least one hour. Why? Warm cake is soft and might break when you remove it from the pan. Plus, any frosting you put on top will melt.

Rotating pans in the oven. The trick to avoiding lopsided cakes is to rotate your pan halfway through the baking time (which means turning it back to front). If you're using more than one rack in the oven, it's a good idea to switch the position of the pans, too.

Filling muffin pans. An ice cream scoop with a thumb release is the perfect way to measure cupcake batter with the least amount of mess.

Filling round cake pans. To get an even amount of batter into each cake pan, use a 1-cup measuring cup to dole out the batter one scoop at a time, alternating pans.

WHEN IS IT DONE?
Cakes and cupcakes are done when you can lightly press the top with your finger and the cake springs back. Better yet, complete the ultimate test: Insert a toothpick into the middle. If it comes out clean, your cake is ready to come out of the oven.

STORING
Keep cakes and cupcakes in an airtight container for up to 5 days. You can also freeze unfrosted cupcakes: Just pop them in an airtight container (don't forget to label it!) and freeze for up to a month. Thaw them overnight in the refrigerator.

BANANA UPSIDE-DOWN CAKE

This is one of those cakes that gets more beautiful when you flip it upside down!

 NUT-FREE | SERVES 9 | PREP TIME 10 MINUTES | BAKE TIME 55 MINUTES

TOOLS/EQUIPMENT
9-by-9-inch square baking pan

Measuring cups and spoons

Rubber spatula

Stand mixer fitted with paddle attachment or large mixing bowl and electric mixer

INGREDIENTS
8 tablespoons (1 stick) salted butter

3 bananas, halved lengthwise

1⅓ cups all-purpose flour

1 cup lightly packed brown sugar

2 teaspoons baking powder

½ teaspoon ground cinnamon

½ cup granulated sugar

½ cup apple juice from concentrate

1 teaspoon vanilla extract

1 large egg

1. **Preheat the oven to 350°F.**
Add the butter to the baking pan and place the pan in the oven to melt the butter as the oven heats up.

2. **Remove the hot pan from the oven.**
When the butter is completely melted, carefully pour it into the mixing bowl. Keep the oven on.

3. **Arrange the bananas.**
Arrange the sliced bananas, cut-side down, in a single layer in the pan.

4. **Mix the batter.**
In the mixing bowl, add the flour, brown sugar, baking powder, cinnamon, granulated sugar, apple juice, vanilla, and egg to the butter. Mix on medium speed for 3 minutes. Carefully pour the batter over the bananas in the pan, using a rubber spatula to smooth it out if needed.

5. **Bake.**

Transfer the pan to the preheated oven. Bake the cake for 50 to 55 minutes, until a toothpick inserted in the center comes out clean.

6. **Flip the cake.**

Remove the pan from the oven. Run a knife around the outside edge of the pan to loosen the cake. Place a plate upside down on top of the pan. Holding both the plate and the pan with potholders, very carefully flip the pan over and place it on the counter. Slowly remove the cake pan, letting any juices drizzle back down on the cake.

7. **Let cool.**

Let the cake cool before serving (the bananas will be very hot). This cake will keep in an airtight container in the refrigerator for up to 5 days.

APPLE CIDER–DOUGHNUT CAKE

This cake is perfect for any occasion, from a tea party to an (extra) special breakfast!

 NUT-FREE   SERVES 12   PREP TIME 10 MINUTES   BAKE TIME 45 MINUTES

TOOLS/EQUIPMENT
9-by-13-inch baking pan
Mixing bowl
Measuring cups and spoons
Rubber spatula
Wire rack
Pastry brush

INGREDIENTS
2 tablespoons salted butter, plus more for greasing

3½ cups all-purpose flour, plus 2 teaspoons for dusting pan

1½ cups granulated sugar, plus 2 teaspoons for topping

2 tablespoons ground cinnamon, plus 1 teaspoon for topping

1½ teaspoons baking powder

½ teaspoon baking soda

½ teaspoon salt

1 cup apple cider

1 cup unsweetened applesauce

¾ cup canola oil

3 large eggs

2 teaspoons vanilla extract

1. **Preheat the oven to 350°F.**
   Grease the pan with butter. Sprinkle 2 teaspoons of flour in the pan and shake the pan until completely coated with flour. Discard the excess flour.

2. **Combine the dry ingredients.**
   In the mixing bowl, combine the remaining 3½ cups of flour, 1½ cups of sugar, 2 tablespoons of cinnamon, the baking powder, baking soda, and salt.

3. **Add the wet ingredients.**
   Add the apple cider, applesauce, oil, eggs, and vanilla. Mix with a spatula just until combined.

4. **Bake.**
   Pour the batter into the prepared cake pan. Transfer the pan to the oven. Bake the cake for 45 minutes, until a toothpick inserted into the center comes out clean.

ASK AN ADULT to butter and flour the pan for you.

5. **Sprinkle with the cinnamon sugar.**

   Remove the cake from the oven and place the pan on a wire rack. In a small bowl, combine the remaining cinnamon and sugar. In another small bowl, melt the remaining 2 tablespoons of butter in the microwave (heat for 20 seconds). Using the pastry brush, coat the top of the cake with the melted butter. Sprinkle with the cinnamon sugar.

6. **Let cool completely before slicing and serving.**

   You can serve the cake right from the pan. This cake will keep in an airtight container in the refrigerator for up to 5 days.

PINK LEMONADE LAYER CAKE

The only question about this pink and yellow cake is whether it's more wonderful to eat or look at!

 NUT-FREE — SERVES 12 — PREP TIME 10 MINUTES — BAKE TIME 25 MINUTES

TOOLS/EQUIPMENT
2 (9-inch) round cake pans
Measuring cups and spoons
Stand mixer fitted with whisk attachment or mixing bowl and electric mixer
Whisk
Rubber spatula
Mixing bowl
Wire rack

FOR THE CAKE
¾ cup (1½ sticks) salted butter, cut into 12 equal pieces, plus more for greasing
2½ cups all-purpose flour, plus 2 teaspoons for dusting the pan
1½ cups granulated sugar
½ teaspoon salt
2½ teaspoons baking powder
4 large eggs
¾ cup frozen pink lemonade concentrate
Zest of 2 lemons
½ cup milk
Pink food coloring
1 batch Vanilla Buttercream Frosting (page 117)
Yellow food coloring

1. **Preheat the oven to 350°F.**
Grease the pan with butter. Sprinkle 2 teaspoons of flour into the pan and shake it until the pan is completely coated with flour. Discard the excess flour.

2. **Mix the dry ingredients.**
In the mixing bowl, whisk together the 2½ cups of flour, sugar, salt, and baking powder.

3. **Add the butter.**
With the mixer on low speed, add the ¾ cup of butter, one piece at a time. Increase the speed to medium, and mix for about 1 minute, until the mixture looks crumbly. Stop partway through to scrape down the sides of the mixing bowl with a rubber spatula if needed. ≫

TIP For different color cakes, use limeade for green and regular lemonade for yellow. You can switch up your frosting color, too!

4. **Mix the wet ingredients.**
In a separate bowl, whisk together the eggs, lemonade concentrate, lemon zest, and milk.

5. **Add half the egg mixture at a time.**
Set the mixer on low speed. Gradually mix in half of the egg mixture to the flour mixture. Increase the speed to medium. Mix for about 30 seconds. Scrape the bowl again. Pour in the remaining egg mixture. Mix again for about 30 seconds.

6. **Add the food coloring.**
Gradually add drops of food coloring until you reach the color you want.

7. **Bake.**
Pour the cake batter into the prepared baking pans. Transfer the pans to the preheated oven. Bake the cake for about 25 minutes (rotating the pans halfway through), until a toothpick inserted into the center comes out clean.

ASK AN ADULT to help you grease and flour the pans and to put the pans in and out of the hot oven. You may also want to ask for help removing the cakes from the pans.

8. **Let cool.**

   Remove the pans from the oven. Let the cakes cool in the pans for about 10 minutes. To remove the cakes from the pans, gently run a butter knife around the outer edge of each cake. One at a time, carefully invert each cake onto the cooling rack and let cool completely, about 1 hour.

9. **Make the frosting.**

   While the cake is cooling, make the frosting (see page 117 for instructions). Mix in drops of yellow food coloring until you reach the color you want.

10. **Decorate.**

    Transfer one of your cooled cakes to a cake stand or platter. Using a knife, cover the top with about ½ cup of the frosting. Then carefully place the remaining cake on top. Use the remaining frosting to cover the top and sides of the cake. This cake will keep in an airtight container in the refrigerator for up to 5 days.

OLD-FASHIONED CHOCOLATE CAKE

Moist and rich, this chocolate cake is the perfect way to celebrate—and you only need one bowl to make it.

 NUT-FREE | SERVES 10 | PREP TIME 10 MINUTES | BAKE TIME 35 MINUTES

TOOLS/EQUIPMENT

2 (9-inch) round cake pans
Measuring cups and spoons
Stand mixer fitted with
    paddle attachment
    or mixing bowl and
    electric mixer
Wooden spoon
Rubber spatula
Wire rack

INGREDIENTS

2 tablespoons salted butter
1¾ cups flour, plus
    2 teaspoons for dusting
    the pans
2 cups granulated sugar
1 cup unsweetened
    cocoa powder
1½ teaspoons baking powder
1½ teaspoons baking soda
1 teaspoon salt
2 large eggs
1 cup buttermilk
½ cup vegetable oil
2 teaspoons vanilla extract
1 cup hot water
1 batch Chocolate Frosting
    (page 119)
Yellow food coloring

1. **Preheat the oven to 350°F.**
Grease the inside of the cake pans with the butter. Sprinkle 1 teaspoon of flour into each pan and shake until the pan is completely coated with flour. Discard any excess flour.

2. **Add the dry ingredients.**
In the mixing bowl, combine the sugar, 1¾ cups of flour, cocoa, baking powder, baking soda, and salt.

3. **Add the wet ingredients.**
Add the eggs, buttermilk, oil, and vanilla. Beat the mixture for 2 minutes, until smooth.

4. **Finish mixing.**
Add the hot water. Using a wooden spoon, stir until the water is just incorporated, about 5 times. >>

TIP No buttermilk? No problem. You can make buttermilk by adding 1 teaspoon of vinegar to 1 cup of regular milk. Let it sit for 2 minutes. Bam! You've got buttermilk.

5. **Bake.**

With a rubber spatula, divide the batter evenly into the prepared pans. Transfer the pans to the oven. Bake the cakes for 30 to 35 minutes (rotating the pans halfway through), until a toothpick inserted into the center comes out clean.

6. **Let cool.**

Remove the pans from the oven. Let the cakes cool in the pans for about 10 minutes. To remove the cakes from the pans, gently run a butter knife around the outer edge of each cake. One at a time, carefully invert each layer onto the cooling rack and let cool completely, about 1 hour.

7. **Make the frosting.**

While the cake is cooling, make the frosting (see page 119 for instructions).

8. **Decorate.**
    Transfer one of your cooled cakes to a cake stand or platter. Using a knife, cover the top with about ½ cup of the frosting. Then carefully place the remaining cake on top. Use the remaining frosting to cover the top and sides of the cake. This cake will keep in an airtight container in the refrigerator for up to 1 week.

FRUIT-FILLED TRIPLE VANILLA CUPCAKES

These classic vanilla cupcakes are perfectly matched with any buttercream frosting, but it's the surprise you find inside that you'll love the most.

 NUT-FREE | MAKES 12 CUPCAKES | PREP TIME 10 MINUTES | BAKE TIME 20 MINUTES

TOOLS/EQUIPMENT

12-cup muffin pan

Baking cups (paper or silicone)

Stand mixer fitted with paddle attachment or mixing bowl and electric mixer

Rubber spatula

Measuring cups and spoons

Ice cream scoop with thumb release

Small knife

Wire rack

INGREDIENTS

¾ cup (1½ sticks) salted butter, very soft

1½ cups granulated sugar

3 teaspoons vanilla extract

2 large eggs

2½ cups all-purpose flour

2½ teaspoons baking powder

1¼ cups milk

2 tablespoons strawberry jam or fruit spread

1 batch frosting of your choice (pages 117 to 119)

1. **Preheat the oven to 350°F.**
   Line the pan with the baking cups.

2. **Cream the butter and sugar.**
   In the mixing bowl, combine the butter and sugar. Beat on medium speed until light and fluffy, about 2 minutes, stopping to scrape down the sides of the mixing bowl with a rubber spatula if needed.

3. **Add the wet ingredients.**
   Mix in the vanilla. Add the eggs, one at a time, mixing well after each addition.

4. **Add the dry ingredients.**
   Mix in the flour and baking powder.

5. **Add the milk.**
   With the mixer running, slowly add the milk and mix just until combined. >>

ASK AN ADULT to help move the pans in and out of the hot oven and cut the holes in the cupcakes.

6. **Bake.**

   Using an ice cream scoop, fill the prepared muffin cups three-quarters full of batter. Transfer the pan to the preheated oven. Bake the cupcakes for 18 to 20 minutes, until a toothpick inserted into the center comes out clean.

7. **Make frosting.**

   While the cupcakes are baking, make the frosting of your choice (see instructions on pages 117 to 119).

8. **Let cool.**

   Remove the pan from the oven. Let the cupcakes cool in the pan for about 5 minutes, then transfer cupcakes to the wire rack to cool completely.

9. **Cut holes for the filling.**
Using a small knife, cut a hole about the size of a quarter in the top of each cupcake, being careful to keep the holes in one piece and not to cut all the way through. Reserve the cake you cut out.

10. **Add the filling.**
Fill each cupcake with about ½ teaspoon of jam. Replace the reserved cake and press down gently.

11. **Decorate.**
Spread frosting on top of each cupcake. You can also add any candy sprinkles or decorations you like. These cupcakes will keep in an airtight container in the refrigerator for up to 5 days.

FRUITY CEREAL CUPCAKES

Have a sweet tooth? You'll love these colorful confections. Bonus: You can eat the leftover cereal for breakfast!

 NUT-FREE | MAKES 12 CUPCAKES | PREP TIME 10 MINUTES | BAKE TIME 18 MINUTES

TOOLS/EQUIPMENT

12-cup muffin pan

Baking cups (paper or silicone)

Stand mixer fitted with paddle attachment or mixing bowl and electric mixer

Measuring cups and spoons

Rubber spatula

Ice cream scoop with thumb release

Wire rack

FOR THE CUPCAKES

½ cup (1 stick) salted butter, very soft

1 cup granulated sugar

1 cup milk

3 large eggs

2 teaspoons vanilla extract

3 cups all-purpose flour

1 tablespoon baking powder

½ teaspoon salt

½ cup Fruity Pebbles™ cereal, plus more for decorating

1 batch Vanilla Buttercream Frosting (page 117)

1. **Preheat the oven to 375°F.**
Line the muffin pan with baking cups.

2. **Cream the butter and sugar.**
In the mixing bowl, combine the butter and sugar. Beat on medium speed until light and fluffy, about 2 minutes, stopping to scrape down the sides of the mixing bowl with the rubber spatula if needed.

3. **Add the wet ingredients.**
Add the milk, eggs, and vanilla to the butter mixture. Beat until combined, about 30 seconds.

4. **Add the dry ingredients.**
Add the flour, baking powder, and salt. Beat again, just until combined, about 10 seconds. Using the rubber spatula, gently stir in the Fruity Pebbles™, being sure to scoop up the batter from the very bottom of the bowl and along the sides.

5. **Bake.**

   Using the ice cream scoop, fill each muffin cup two-thirds full. Transfer the pan to the preheated oven. Bake the cupcakes for 15 to 18 minutes, until a toothpick inserted into the center comes out clean.

6. **Let cool.**

   Remove the pan from the oven. Let the cupcakes cool in the pan for 5 minutes, then transfer the cupcakes to a wire rack to cool completely (for about an hour) before frosting.

7. **Make the frosting.**

   While the cupcakes are cooling, make the frosting (see page 117 for instructions).

8. **Decorate.**

   Spread a large dollop of frosting onto the top of each cupcake. Sprinkle with additional Fruity Pebbles™. These cupcakes will keep in an airtight container in the refrigerator for up to 5 days (wait until just before serving to top with the Fruity Pebbles™).

COOKIES AND CREAM CUPCAKES

Hopelessly decadent, these Oreo-studded cupcakes are the way to any cookies-and-cream lover's heart.

 NUT-FREE | MAKES 24 CUPCAKES | PREP TIME 1 HOUR 10 MINUTES | BAKE TIME 20 MINUTES

TOOLS/EQUIPMENT
2 (12-cup) muffin pans
Baking cups (silicone or paper)
Zip-top bag
Rolling pin
Stand mixer fitted with
    paddle attachment
    or mixing bowl and
    electric mixer
Measuring cups and spoons
Rubber spatula
Ice cream scoop with
    thumb release
Wire rack

FOR THE CUPCAKES
49 Oreo cookies
1½ cups granulated sugar
½ cup vegetable oil
3 large eggs
1 tablespoon vanilla extract
½ cup sour cream
2½ cups all-purpose flour
3 teaspoons baking powder
1 teaspoon salt
1¼ cups milk
1 batch Vanilla Buttercream
    Frosting (page 117)

1. **Preheat the oven to 350°F.**
Grease or line the muffins pans with silicone or paper baking cups.

2. **Crush the cookies.**
Put 25 cookies in the zip-top bag and, using the rolling pin, crush them into small pieces. You should have about 3 cups. Set aside.

3. **Make the batter.**
In the mixing bowl, combine the sugar, oil, eggs, and vanilla. Beat for 2 minutes. Add the sour cream. Beat again until well combined, about 30 seconds.

4. **Add the dry ingredients.**
Add the flour, baking powder, and salt. Mix well. While mixing on low speed, gradually add the milk. Increase the speed to medium and mix for 30 seconds.

5. **Add the crushed cookies.**
Using the rubber spatula, fold 2 cups of the crushed cookies into the batter until evenly distributed. Put aside the remaining 1 cup of crushed cookies for the frosting. >>

ASK AN ADULT to help move the pans in and out of the hot oven, and to rotate the pans halfway through the baking time.

6. **Bake.**

   Using the ice cream scoop, fill each muffin cup three-quarters full. Transfer the pan to the preheated oven. Bake the cupcakes for 18 to 20 minutes (rotating the pans halfway through), until a toothpick inserted in the center comes out clean.

7. **Let cool.**

   Remove the pans from the oven. Let the cupcakes cool in the pan for about 5 minutes, then transfer to the wire rack and let them cool completely.

8. **Make the frosting.**

   While the cupcakes are cooling, make the frosting (see page 117 for instructions). Add the reserved 1 cup of crushed Oreos and mix well.

9. **Decorate.**

   When the cupcakes are completely cooled, smooth a large dollop of frosting on top of each. Arrange a whole Oreo on top. (Without the Oreo on top, these cupcakes will keep in an airtight container in the refrigerator for up to 5 days.)

VANILLA BUTTERCREAM FROSTING

This is a wonderful all-purpose vanilla frosting. Plus you can dress it up by adding extras like candy sprinkles, crumbled cookies, or your favorite cereal.

 NUT-FREE | MAKES 3 TO 4 CUPS | PREP TIME 10 MINUTES

TOOLS/EQUIPMENT
Stand mixer fitted with
   paddle attachment
   or mixing bowl and
   electric mixer
Measuring cups and spoons
Rubber spatula

INGREDIENTS
1½ cups (3 sticks) salted
   butter, very soft
8 ounces (1 stick) cream
   cheese, at room
   temperature
2½ cups confectioners' sugar
2 tablespoons heavy cream
1 tablespoon vanilla extract

TIP Use immediately
or store in an airtight
container in the refrigerator for up to 2 weeks. If
you refrigerate it, allow
the frosting to warm up
to room temperature
before using.

1. **Mix the butter, cream cheese, and sugar.**
   In the mixing bowl, on medium speed, beat together the butter, cream cheese, and confectioners' sugar until light and fluffy, 1 to 2 minutes, stopping to scrape down the sides of the bowl with the rubber spatula as needed.

2. **Reduce the mixer speed to low.**
   Gradually add the cream and vanilla, and beat just until incorporated. Then increase the speed to medium-high. Beat until the frosting is light and fluffy, 1 to 2 minutes.

STRAWBERRY FROSTING

Loaded with fresh fruit, there's no sweeter frosting. Plus, the same recipe works for other fruit, too. Try cherries, peaches, or raspberries!

 NUT-FREE | MAKES 2 CUPS | PREP TIME 10 MINUTES

TOOLS/EQUIPMENT
Measuring cups and spoons
Stand mixer fitted with
     paddle attachment
     or mixing bowl and
     electric mixer
Rubber spatula

INGREDIENTS
6 tablespoons (¾ stick)
     salted butter, very soft
¼ cup finely diced hulled
     strawberries (about 3 to
     4 strawberries)
3 cups confectioners' sugar
1 teaspoon vanilla
1 tablespoon strawberry jam

TIP Set the butter out
overnight to get it soft.
If fresh from the fridge,
warm it in the microwave
for 15 seconds.

ASK AN ADULT to help
you hull and chop the
strawberries.

1. **Cream the butter and strawberries.**
   In the mixing bowl, on medium speed, beat together the butter and strawberries until the berries start to release their juice and they mix into the butter, about 1 minute.

2. **Add the confectioner's sugar and vanilla.**
   Turn the mixer off and add the sugar ½ cup at a time, mixing on low between additions. Scrape down the bowl with a rubber spatula and mix in the vanilla.

3. **Add the jam.**
   Beat again until the frosting is pink with little bits of red strawberry peaking through. Use immediately or store in an airtight container in the refrigerator for up to 5 days. If you refrigerate it, allow the frosting to warm up to room temperature before using.

CHOCOLATE FROSTING

It takes only a couple of minutes to make this decadent, thick, and chocolatey frosting.

 NUT-FREE | MAKES 2 CUPS | PREP TIME 15 MINUTES | COOK TIME 1 MINUTE

TOOLS/EQUIPMENT

Measuring cups and spoons
Microwave-safe bowl
Rubber spatula

INGREDIENTS

1 cup chocolate chips
(semi-sweet or milk
chocolate)
1 cup full-fat Greek yogurt

TIP Use immediately or store in an airtight container in the refrigerator for up to 2 weeks. If you refrigerate it, allow the frosting to warm up to room temperature before using.

ASK AN ADULT to help you melt the chocolate.

1. **Melt the chocolate.**
   Pour the chocolate chips into the microwave-safe bowl. Heat in the microwave for 30 seconds. Pause for a few seconds and then heat for another 30 seconds. Using the spatula, stir well. If needed, heat for an additional 15 seconds, until the chocolate is completely melted. Set aside to cool slightly, about 5 minutes.

2. **Add the yogurt.**
   Mix in the yogurt until the frosting is smooth and evenly colored.

APPLE CROSTATA, PAGE 139

CHAPTER FIVE

PIES AND TARTS

There's nothing as flaky and sweet as a piece of pie! This chapter includes seasonal favorites—from a summery Rainbow Fruit Tart to the Chocolate-Pecan Pie my kids beg for every fall—made simple. Adults will need to help with a bit of chopping, plus handling hot pans coming in and out of the oven.

RECIPES

TIPS AND TECHNIQUES

Making pie dough is so much easier than you think. Trust me, I *always* used to buy mine at the store until I perfected this recipe. Buttery, flaky, and easy enough for cooks of any age, all you need is a pastry bender and a bowl. Most treats from this section use the same pie dough, and you'll use the following techniques:

Cutting in butter. The main ingredients of pie dough are flour and cold butter. To combine the two, use a pastry blender (which looks like a rounded claw with a handle). Here's how the pastry blender works: Put the butter and flour in a bowl, then press down on the butter and twist. Repeat, repeat, repeat until your mixture looks like sand. Believe it or not, that's exactly what you want.

Cooling dough. Butter warms up during the cutting-in process so you'll need to chill the dough in the fridge to let it firm up before you roll it out. This usually takes about 20 minutes. If you chill the dough longer, leave it on the counter for 10 to 15 minutes so it can warm up slightly. The perfect temperature—colder than room temperature but not as cold as the fridge—will make your dough easy to work with. If it feels too hard to roll, it's too cold.

Rolling dough. Always work on a clean, flat surface. Sprinkle it with a handful of flour then set your dough on top. Rub a little flour on your rolling pin and start rolling. Roll in one direction then another. This is how you'll achieve a round shape. Aim for dough that's an even ¼ inch thick (about as wide as a chopstick).

Moving dough. When it's time to transfer your rolled dough to a pie pan, gently roll it up on the rolling pin. Move the rolling pin over the pie pan and unroll.

WHEN IS IT DONE?
When it comes to pastry, it's all about color on the crust. You're looking for a very light golden brown on the edges. For custard pies (like lemon, pumpkin, or pecan), the filling should be just set—not too firm and not too jiggly. The filling in fruit pies should look bubbly.

STORING
It's not hard to make pie dough, but I still like to make a couple of batches at once. That way there's less cleanup next time.

- To store pie dough for up to 1 week, shape the dough into a disc, wrap it in plastic, and refrigerate.
- To store the pie dough for even longer, put your plastic-wrapped dough inside a freezer-safe bag and you can freeze for up to 4 months. Be sure to label and write the date on the bag. (You'd be surprised at how different it looks inside the freezer!) When you're ready to use the dough, put it in the refrigerator over-night to thaw out.

Bring the dough to room temperature before using (20 minutes on the counter ought to do it). This allows the butter in the dough to warm up so the dough is easier to roll out.

PERFECT PIE DOUGH

With this recipe you'll be able to make almost every pie in this chapter. The key to flaky pastry is mixing the butter into the flour until the mixture looks like coarse sand. Using a pastry blender makes the job easy, but two or three pulses in a food processor would also work.

 NUT-FREE | MAKES 2 PIECRUSTS | (ENOUGH FOR 1 DOUBLE-CRUST PIE) | PREP TIME 40 MINUTES

TOOLS/EQUIPMENT
Mixing bowl
Rubber spatula
Measuring cups and spoons
Pastry blender or food
    processor

INGREDIENTS
2½ cups all-purpose flour
1 teaspoon granulated sugar
½ teaspoon salt
1 cup (2 sticks) chilled
    salted butter, cut into
    16 even pieces
4 tablespoons ice water, plus
    more if needed

TIP To store homemade pie dough in the freezer, wrap in plastic, then place the dough inside a freezer-safe zip-top bag for up to 4 months.

1. **Mix the dry ingredients.**
   In the mixing bowl, using the spatula, stir together the flour, sugar, and salt.

2. **Cut in the butter.**
   Using the pastry blender, food processor, or your fingers, work the butter into the flour until the mixture looks like coarse sand.

3. **Add the water.**
   Gradually add the water and, using your hands, mix until a dough forms. If it's too crumbly to form a ball, add 1 tablespoon of water and continue mixing. If it's still too crumbly, add another tablespoon of water. When you can form a smooth ball, the dough is ready.

4. **Chill the dough.**
   Cut the ball of dough in half. Flatten each half into a disc. Wrap each disc in plastic wrap and refrigerate for at least 20 minutes. Your dough is now ready to use.

BLACKBERRY PIE POPPERS

Pie poppers are small, single-serving pies that you can pop in your mouth! These are filled with sweetened blackberries, but you can use any fresh or frozen fruit you like. You can also substitute milk for the cream, if needed.

	NUT-FREE	MAKES 20 POPPERS	PREP TIME 30 MINUTES	BAKE TIME 30 MINUTES

TOOLS/EQUIPMENT

Baking sheet
Parchment paper or silicone baking mat
Large mixing bowl
Measuring cups and spoons
Rolling pin
Ice cube tray
Kitchen towel
Knife or pizza cutter
Small bowl
Pastry brush

INGREDIENTS

1 batch Perfect Pie Dough (page 124)
3 cups blackberries (fresh or thawed from frozen)
½ cup lightly packed brown sugar
½ cup all-purpose flour, plus more for rolling
2 tablespoons heavy cream
2 tablespoons cinnamon sugar

1. **Prepare the pie dough.**
Follow the recipe on page 124. (You'll need both discs for this recipe.)

2. **Preheat the oven to 400°F.**
Line the baking sheet with parchment paper or a silicone mat. Bring the pie dough to room temperature before using (about 20 minutes on the counter should do it).

3. **Prepare the filling.**
In the mixing bowl, combine the blackberries, brown sugar, and flour.

4. **Roll out the dough.**
Dust a clean work surface with flour. Using a rolling pin, roll out each disc of dough to a rectangle about ¼ inch thick. Transfer one of the rectangles of dough to the ice cube tray by carefully rolling the dough onto the rolling pin and unrolling it onto the top of the ice cube tray. Cover the remaining dough with a kitchen towel. >>

TIP Don't throw away any leftover pastry! Roll any leftover dough ¼ inch thick, cut it into strips, and sprinkle with cinnamon sugar. Bake on a separate baking sheet for 10 to 12 minutes, until crispy. #yum

TIP Frozen blackberries are always in season (and affordable!), but they'll have a little more juice than fresh so you need to coat them in flour before using. Pour berries into a small bowl and sprinkle with ¼ cup of flour. Gently stir to coat, then proceed with step 3.

5. **Make the pockets.**
Using your fingers, gently press down into each cube to form a small pocket. Fill each pocket with 1 teaspoon of the blackberry mixture (1 or 2 blackberries, depending on their size). Transfer the remaining rolled-out dough to the ice cube tray to make a top. Press down along the edges with the rolling pin. The extra crust should fall away.

6. **Trim the pockets.**
Lightly dust a clean work surface with flour. Quickly flip the ice cube tray upside down. Using a knife or pizza cutter, cut between the pockets to separate them. Place each filled pocket on the prepared baking sheet, spacing them about 2 inches apart.

7. **Bake.**
Using a pastry brush, coat each pocket with cream. Combine the cinnamon and sugar in a small bowl, then sprinkle over the tops. Bake in the preheated oven for 25 to 30 minutes, until golden brown.

8. **Let cool.**
Remove the pan from the oven. Let the poppers cool on the pan for 10 minutes, then serve. Poppers will keep in an airtight container in the refrigerator for up to 5 days.

MINI BLUEBERRY HAND PIES

Flaky little pies you can eat with your hands? Yes, please. If you aren't a fan of blueberries, swap in your favorite jam of any flavor.

 NUT-FREE | MAKES 12 MINI PIES | PREP TIME 30 MINUTES | BAKE TIME 12 MINUTES

TOOLS/EQUIPMENT
Baking sheet
Parchment paper
Measuring cups and spoons
Rolling pin
3-inch round cookie cutter
  or drinking glass
Fork
Small bowl
Pastry brush
Wire rack

INGREDIENTS
1 batch Perfect Pie Dough
  (page 124)
All-purpose flour, for rolling
1 cup blueberry jam
¼ cup heavy cream

1. **Prepare the pie dough.**
Follow the recipe on page 124. (You'll need both discs of dough for this recipe.) Bring the dough to room temperature before using.

2. **Preheat the oven to 400°F.**
Line the baking sheet with parchment paper.

3. **Roll out the pie dough.**
Sprinkle a teaspoon of flour on a clean work surface. Sprinkle the dough with flour. Using your rolling pin, flatten the dough: Roll in one direction, rotate the pin, and then roll the other way. Repeat until your dough stretches out to about ¼ inch thick.

4. **Cut out circles.**
Using a 3-inch round cookie cutter or a drinking glass, press circles into your first disc of dough. When you've cut all the circles you can, gather the remaining dough, roll it out again, and cut more circles. You should have 12 rounds total, which makes 6 hand pies. To make more rounds, repeat steps 3 and 4 with the second disc of pie dough. >>

TIP If you didn't end up with 12 rounds, don't worry. You just need an even number of rounds so every pie has a lid.

TIP Make these mini pies a little more special by using cookie cutters to shape them. Try a pumpkin-shaped cookie cutter and apricot jam filling for Halloween or a star-shaped cookie cutter with raspberry jam filling for Christmas. The combinations are endless.

5. **Add the filling.**
Transfer 12 rounds to the prepared baking sheet. Top each with about 1 teaspoon of blueberry jam in the center.

6. **Cover with the lids.**
Use the remaining rounds of dough to top each of the 12 pies. Using a fork, press together the edges to seal the pies all the way around.

7. **Brush the tops with the cream.**
Pour the cream into a small bowl. Using a pastry brush, lightly coat the top of each pie with cream.

8. **Bake.**
Transfer the baking sheet to the preheated oven. Bake the pies for 10 to 12 minutes, until golden brown on top.

9. **Let cool.**
Remove the pan from the oven. Let the pies cool on the pan for 5 minutes, then transfer to the wire rack to cool completely. These pies will keep in an airtight container at room temperature for up to 3 days.

MINI PUMPKIN PIES

These handheld mini pumpkin pies may become your new holiday tradition. They're full of fall flavors and trust me, you won't be able to eat just one!

	NUT-FREE	MAKES 18 MINI PIES	PREP TIME 10 MINUTES	BAKE TIME 20 MINUTES

TOOLS/EQUIPMENT
2 (12-cup) muffin pans

Stand mixer fitted with paddle attachment or mixing bowl and electric mixer

Rolling pin

3-inch round cookie cutter or drinking glass

Wire racks

INGREDIENTS
Butter, for greasing the pan

1 batch Perfect Pie Dough (page 124)

2 large eggs

8 ounces (1 stick) cream cheese, at room temperature

½ cup lightly packed brown sugar

1 cup canned pumpkin purée (not pumpkin pie filling)

1 teaspoon vanilla extract

2 teaspoons pumpkin pie spice

All-purpose flour, for rolling

Whipped cream, for serving

1. **Preheat the oven to 350°F.**
Grease the muffin pans.

2. **Prepare the piecrust.**
Follow the recipe on page 124. (You'll need both discs of dough for this recipe.) Bring the pie dough to room temperature before using (about 20 minutes on the counter should do it).

3. **Make the filling.**
In the mixing bowl, beat together the eggs, cream cheese, brown sugar, pumpkin, vanilla, and pumpkin pie spice until smooth.

4. **Roll out the piecrust.**
Lightly sprinkle some flour on a clean work surface. Using the rolling pin, flatten each portion of dough until it's about ¼ inch thick. >>

ASK AN ADULT to help you rotate the pans in the hot oven.

5. **Assemble the mini pies.**

Using a cookie cutter or drinking glass, cut out 18 rounds. Place one round of dough in each muffin cup. Using your fingers, press down on the center, and gently pat the dough into the bottom and up the sides. Fill each cup with about 3 tablespoons of the pumpkin mixture.

6. **Bake.**

Transfer the pans to the preheated oven. Bake the pies for 15 to 20 minutes, until the pumpkin is set and the edges are slightly golden brown. Switch the position of the pans halfway through (move the top pan to the bottom, and vice versa; also rotate the pans back to front).

7. **Let cool.**

Remove the pans from the oven, place on wire racks, and let cool completely (about 30 minutes).

8. **Top with whipped cream.**

To serve, remove the pies from the pans by gently pressing down on one side of the crust. Add a dollop of whipped cream to the top of each pie. If you're making these pies ahead of time, cover and store them in the fridge for up to 4 days. Don't add the whipped cream until you're ready to serve.

PEACHES AND CREAM PIE

This pie tastes just like a peach creamsicle. The best news: You use frozen peaches (which are already peeled and sliced), so you can enjoy them year-round.

     NUT-FREE   SERVES 8   PREP TIME 20 MINUTES   BAKE TIME 50 MINUTES

TOOLS/EQUIPMENT
Baking sheet
Parchment paper
Rolling pin
9-inch pie pan
Fork
Medium mixing bowl
Whisk
Wire rack

INGREDIENTS
½ batch Perfect Pie Dough (page 124)

3 tablespoons all-purpose flour, plus more for rolling

3 cups frozen sliced peaches, thawed

2 large eggs

½ cup lightly packed brown sugar

1 cup sour cream

1 teaspoon ground cinnamon

1. **Prepare the piecrust.**
Follow the recipe on page 124. (This recipe only requires 1 disc of pie dough, so freeze the other disc for another time.) Bring the pie dough to room temperature before using (about 20 minutes on the counter should do it).

2. **Preheat oven to 425°F.**
Line the baking sheet with parchment paper.

3. **Roll out the dough.**
Lightly sprinkle some flour on a clean work surface. Using the rolling pin, flatten the dough to make an 11-inch circle that's about ¼ inch thick. Transfer the dough to the pie pan by carefully rolling the dough onto the rolling pin and unrolling it over the pie pan. With your fingers, press the dough into the bottom of the pie pan. Fold the overhanging edges of dough up around the top of the pie pan. Using the tines of a fork, press all around the edges so the dough stays in place.

4. **Add the peaches.**
Place the pie pan on the prepared baking sheet. (This helps catch any drips in the oven.) Arrange the peach slices in an even layer on top of the dough.

5. **Make the filling.**
In a medium bowl, whisk the eggs until frothy. Add the 3 tablespoons of flour, the brown sugar, sour cream, and cinnamon. Whisk again until well blended, about 30 seconds. Carefully pour the prepared filling over the peaches.

6. **Bake.**
Transfer the pan to the preheated oven. Bake for 15 minutes. Reduce the oven temperature to 375°F. Bake for another 35 minutes.

7. **Let cool.**
Remove the pan from the oven and place on a wire rack to cool completely. This pie will keep in an airtight container in the refrigerator for up to 3 days.

CHOCOLATE-PECAN PIE

If you like chocolate, you'll love chocolate-pecan pie. It's sweet and gooey and oh-so-good.

 SERVES 8   PREP TIME 20 MINUTES   BAKE TIME 50 MINUTES

TOOLS/EQUIPMENT
Baking sheet
Parchment paper
Rolling pin
9-inch pie pan
Fork
Stand mixer fitted with
   paddle attachment
   or mixing bowl and
   electric mixer
Rubber spatula
Aluminum foil
Wire rack

INGREDIENTS
½ batch Perfect Pie Dough
   (page 124)
All-purpose flour, for rolling
⅔ cup granulated sugar
⅓ cup salted butter, melted
1 cup corn syrup
3 large eggs
1 cup pecan halves
1 cup semisweet
   chocolate chips
Whipped cream, for serving

1. **Preheat the oven to 375°F.**
Line the baking sheet with parchment paper.

2. **Prepare the pie dough.**
Follow the recipe on page 124. (This recipe only requires 1 disc of pie dough, so freeze the other disc for another time.) Bring the pie dough to room temperature before using (about 20 minutes on the counter should do it).

3. **Roll out the dough.**
Lightly sprinkle some flour on a clean work surface. Using the rolling pin, flatten the dough to make an 11-inch circle that's about ¼ inch thick. Transfer the dough to the pie pan by carefully rolling the dough onto the rolling pin and unrolling it over the pie pan. Fold the overhanging edges of dough up around the top of the pie pan. Using the tines of a fork, press all around the edges so it stays in place. >>

ASK AN ADULT to help you remove the aluminum foil from the piecrust for the last 15 minutes of baking time.

4. **Mix the filling.**
In the mixing bowl, beat together the sugar, butter, corn syrup, and eggs until smooth, about 2 minutes. Using a rubber spatula, fold in the pecans and chocolate chips.

5. **Assemble the pie.**
Place the pie pan on the prepared baking sheet. (This will keep the pan level and catch any drips during baking.) Pour the chocolate mixture into the pie pan. Cover the edges of the pie dough with aluminum foil so it doesn't burn. (You'll remove it for the last 15 minutes of baking.)

6. **Bake.**
Transfer the pan to the preheated oven. Bake the pie for 40 to 50 minutes, until the filling sets and is not too jiggly. Remove the foil for the last 15 minutes of baking.

7. **Let cool.**
Remove the pan from the oven and place on a wire rack to cool for 30 minutes. When cool, refrigerate the pie for at least 2 hours before cutting. (Never put a hot pan directly in the fridge.) Serve with whipped cream. This pie will keep in an airtight container in the refrigerator for up to 5 days.

APPLE CROSTATA

A crostata is an open-faced fruit tart. It's meant to be rustic-looking, and it's my favorite way to make pies. The great thing about this recipe is that you can switch up the fruit filling. We always make one blueberry crostata and one raspberry for the 4th of July.

 SERVES 6 | PREP TIME 20 MINUTES | BAKE TIME 25 MINUTES

TOOLS/EQUIPMENT
Baking sheet
Parchment paper
Rolling pin
Medium mixing bowl
Rubber spatula

INGREDIENTS
½ batch Perfect Pie Dough (page 124)
¼ cup all-purpose flour, plus more for rolling
1½ cups peeled, cored, and sliced apples (3 large apples)
Zest of 1 lemon
¼ cup granulated sugar
¼ teaspoon salt
1 teaspoon ground cinnamon
¼ teaspoon pumpkin pie spice
2 tablespoons salted butter, cut into 4 pieces

1. **Preheat the oven to 450° F.**
Line the baking sheet with parchment paper.

2. **Prepare the pie dough.**
Follow the recipe on page 124. (You'll only need 1 disc of pie dough for this recipe, so freeze the other disc for another time.) Bring the dough to room temperature before using (about 20 minutes on the counter should do it).

3. **Roll out the dough.**
Dust a clean work surface with flour. Using a rolling pin, roll out the dough into a rough circle about ¼ inch thick. It should be around 11 inches wide. Place in the center of the prepared baking sheet.

4. **Prepare the filling.**
In the medium bowl, combine the apples, lemon zest, ¼ cup of flour, the sugar, salt, cinnamon, and pumpkin pie spice. Use your hands to mix, making sure every apple slice is coated in the mixture. >>

ASK AN ADULT to help you peel, core, and slice the apples.

5. **Assemble the crostata.**
Pour the apple mixture into the center of the pastry. (Use a rubber spatula to get all the juices off the bottom and sides of the bowl.) Spread the mixture, leaving a 3-inch border around the edge (about as long as your thumb). Fold the edges of the dough over the apples. You don't want it to cover the fruit completely. It should look like a ring around the apples. Place the four pieces of butter on top of the apples.

6. **Bake.**
Transfer the pan to the preheated oven. Bake the crostata for 20 to 25 minutes, until the filling is bubbly and the crust is golden.

7. **Let cool.**
Remove the pan from the oven. Let the crostata cool on the pan for 10 minutes, then serve. The crostata will keep in an airtight container in the refrigerator for up to 3 days.

LEMON AND BLUEBERRY PUFF PASTRY TART

Puff pastry is kind of magical. The dough starts out flat then transforms into an impossibly light and crispy crust when baked. Add a lemon blueberry filling, and you've got something truly enchanting.

 NUT-FREE | SERVES 8 | PREP TIME 25 MINUTES | BAKE TIME 1 HOUR

TOOLS/EQUIPMENT
Baking sheet
Parchment paper or silicone baking mat
Rolling pin
Fork
Dried beans or pie weights
Large mixing bowl
Whisk

INGREDIENTS
1 sheet of puff pastry
¼ cup granulated sugar
1 large egg
¼ cup heavy cream
Zest and juice of 1 lemon
1 pint blueberries

1. **Preheat the oven to 400°F.**
Line the baking sheet with parchment paper or a silicone mat.

2. **Bake the puff pastry.**
Remove the puff pastry from the package and let it thaw on the counter for 15 minutes, just until soft. Using a rolling pin, flatten out any creases. Transfer the pastry to the prepared baking sheet. Fold over 1 inch of each edge to make a border. (This will be the crust.) Using the fork, poke the pastry all over, about 10 times. Place a second piece of parchment paper over the pastry and cover the center square with the dried beans or pie weights (don't cover the edges). This will help the pastry stay flat during baking. Transfer the pan to the preheated oven. Bake the pastry for 20 minutes. Remove the pan from the oven and let cool for 10 minutes. Keep the oven on. >>

3. **Prepare the filling.**
In the large bowl, whisk together the sugar, egg, cream, and lemon zest and juice until smooth.

4. **Fill the tart.**
When cool, remove the dried beans or pie weights from the pastry. (Don't throw them away. You can reuse them next time!) Pour the prepared filling into the empty crust.

5. **Bake.**
Reduce the oven temperature to 300°F. Place the pan back into the oven. Bake the tart for 35 to 40 minutes, until the filling is set.

6. **Add the blueberries.**
Remove the pan from the oven and let cool for 5 minutes. When cooled slightly, arrange the blueberries on top of the filling.

7. **Let cool.**
Allow the tart to cool for 20 minutes before serving. This tart will keep in the refrigerator for up to 3 hours.

RAINBOW FRUIT TART

Use every color of fruit you can find, including blueberries, raspberries, or sliced strawberries, kiwi, or peaches—in any pattern you like—for this vibrant dessert!

 NUT-FREE | SERVES 8 | PREP TIME 40 MINUTES | BAKE TIME 12 MINUTES

TOOLS/EQUIPMENT
9-inch pie pan
Large bowl
Measuring cups and spoons
Pastry blender or food processor
Wire rack
Stand mixer fitted with paddle attachment or mixing bowl with electric mixer
Rubber spatula
Microwave-safe bowl
Pastry brush

FOR THE CRUST
1½ cups all-purpose flour
½ cup confectioners' sugar
¾ cup (1½ sticks) salted butter, very soft

FOR THE FILLING
8 ounces (1 stick) cream cheese, at room temperature
½ cup granulated sugar
1 teaspoon vanilla extract
2 to 3 cups any combination of fresh fruit
½ cup apricot jam

1. **Preheat the oven to 350°F.**

2. **Make the crust.**
In the large bowl, combine the flour, confectioners' sugar, and butter. Using the pastry blender, food processor, or your fingers, work the butter into the flour mixture until it looks like coarse sand. Using your hands, shape the mixture into a disc.

3. **Bake the crust.**
Using the heels of your palms, press the dough into the bottom of the pie pan, patting until it's even all the way around, then press the dough 1 inch up the sides of the pan. Transfer the pan to the preheated oven. Bake the dough for 10 to 12 minutes, until golden brown. Remove the pan from the oven and place on a wire rack to cool.

4. **Prepare the filling.**
In the mixing bowl, beat together the cream cheese, sugar, and vanilla until smooth. Using a rubber spatula, spread the mixture over the cooled crust. >>

TIP The tart will be easier to cut if you take it out of the fridge a few minutes before you're ready to serve.

ASK AN ADULT to help you slice the fruit.

5. **Add the fruit.**
Arrange the sliced fruit in a rainbow pattern on the crust. Start on the outside edge and work your way in, alternating fruit and colors, until the tart is covered.

6. **Glaze the tart.**
Spoon the jam into a microwave-safe bowl. Heat for 30-second intervals, until the jam is runny. Using a pastry brush, gently coat the fruit with the glaze.

7. **Chill.**
Transfer the tart to the refrigerator and chill for at least 20 minutes before serving. This tart will keep in the fridge for up to 3 hours.

GRANDMA'S CHOCOLATE-HAZELNUT WHOLE-WHEAT TARTS

My family loves these tarts. Try them with this decadent filling or your favorite jam.

 MAKES 24 TARTS **PREP TIME** 20 MINUTES **BAKE TIME** 40 MINUTES

TOOLS/EQUIPMENT
Measuring cups and spoons

Stand mixer fitted with paddle attachment or mixing bowl and electric mixer

2 (12-cup) muffin pans

Wire racks

INGREDIENTS
8 ounces (1 stick) cream cheese, at room temperature

1 cup (2 sticks) salted butter, very soft

2 cups whole-wheat flour

1½ cups chocolate-hazelnut spread

ASK AN ADULT to help you rotate the pans in the hot oven.

1. **Preheat the oven to 350°F.**
   Line the muffin pans with paper baking cups or coat with nonstick cooking spray.

2. **Mix the ingredients.**
   In the mixing bowl, beat the cream cheese, butter, and flour until combined.

3. **Form into tarts.**
   Roll the dough into 2-inch balls with your hands. Place a ball into each cup of the muffin pans. Press down on the dough so it covers the bottom of each cup.

4. **Add the filling.**
   Add 1 tablespoon of chocolate-hazelnut spread to each cup.

5. **Bake.**
   Transfer the pans to the preheated oven. Bake the tarts for 35 to 40 minutes, until the edges look slightly golden.

6. **Let cool.**
   Remove the pans from the oven. After 5 minutes, cool the tarts completely on wire racks. These will keep refrigerated up to 5 days.

BAKED TORTILLA CHIPS, PAGE 175

CHAPTER SIX

SAVORY AND SALTY BREADS AND SNACKS

To me, there's no better smell in all the world than freshly baked bread. And you know what's neat about making bread? You need to use yeast, which is a real live organism! When you add it to a warm liquid, yeast "blooms" and produces carbon dioxide, which is what helps baked goods rise. You'll make bread in this chapter and a bunch of other quick and easy snacks.

RECISES

TIPS AND TECHNIQUES

Working with yeast and making bread dough are easy when you follow a few basic steps.

Proofing yeast. Yeast needs a warm liquid and something sweet in order to "bloom" or grow. That's why most of the recipes in this chapter call for yeast mixed with warm water plus a bit of sugar. After a few minutes, the mixture should become frothy—that's when you know it's ready to use.

Allowing the dough to rise. Baking with yeast requires more time than some of the other recipes in this book. You'll need to wait anywhere from 10 minutes to 1 hour to let the dough double in size. But it's worth it. The final product will be light, fluffy, and delicious.

Flouring your surface. Sprinkle a handful of flour on a clean, flat surface before placing your dough on top. This helps prevent the dough from sticking.

Kneading dough. Most dough starts out sticky. After you add a little extra flour and start kneading it with the heel of your hand, the dough will transform into a smooth ball. It takes a little time, up to about 10 minutes, but when it feels silky you know you've added the right amount of flour and kneaded it enough.

WHEN IS IT DONE?

In general, look for the top or edges of baked goods to turn golden. Also, don't panic if your chips, crackers, or pretzels aren't crispy when they come out of the oven. They'll crisp up as they cool.

STORING

Most dough can be stored in an airtight container in the fridge for up to 1 week or in the freezer for up to 2 months. To work from frozen, simply let the dough thaw out in the fridge overnight. Bring to room temperature before using (about 20 minutes on the counter should do it).

QUICK AND EASY HOMEMADE BREAD

You won't believe how simply this recipe for homemade bread comes together. It's one of my family's favorites.

 NUT-FREE   MAKES 1 LOAF   PREP TIME 35 MINUTES   BAKE TIME 25 MINUTES

TOOLS/EQUIPMENT
Mixing bowl
Whisk
Measuring cups and spoons
Wooden spoon
Loaf pan
Kitchen towel
Wire rack

INGREDIENTS
3¼ cups all-purpose flour, divided
¼ cup granulated sugar
1 (7-ounce) package yeast (2¼ teaspoons)
1 cup warm water (like bathwater)
1 teaspoon salt
¼ cup salted butter, melted
Nonstick baking spray

1. **Mix the dry ingredients.**
In the mixing bowl, whisk together 1 cup of the flour, the sugar, and yeast.

2. **Add the water.**
Pour the warm water over the flour mixture and, using the wooden spoon, stir to combine. Set aside in a warm spot on the counter for 10 minutes.

3. **Add the second cup of flour.**
When the yeast mixture looks puffy, add another 1 cup of flour, the salt, and melted butter. Stir well.

4. **Add the third cup of flour.**
Add another 1 cup of flour. Stir again.

5. **Knead the dough.**
Your dough will be very sticky. Pour ¼ cup of additional flour onto a clean work surface, then put the dough on top. Using your hands, knead the dough: Press down with the heel of your hand, then fold the dough in half. Press down again, then fold. Keep kneading for 10 minutes.

6. **Let the dough rise.**
   Once the dough feels silky, transfer it to a loaf pan coated with nonstick cooking spray. Cover the pan with a clean kitchen towel and place it in a warm spot. Leave for 35 minutes to rise.

7. **Preheat the oven to 375°F.**

8. **Let the dough rise a second time.**
   Punch the dough down with your fist. Cover with the towel and let it rise for 10 minutes longer, while the oven heats.

9. **Bake.**
   Uncover and transfer the pan to the pre-heated oven for 25 minutes, until the bread has pulled away from the sides of the pan and the top is golden brown.

10. **Let cool.**
    Remove the pan from the oven and place on a wire rack to cool. Remove from the pan to slice and serve. The bread will keep in an airtight container for 3 to 5 days.

30-MINUTE DINNER ROLLS

Freshly baked soft and buttery dinner rolls aren't just delicious—they'll make your whole house smell amazing, too.

	NUT-FREE	MAKES 12 ROLLS	PREP TIME 10 MINUTES	BAKE TIME 19 MINUTES

TOOLS/EQUIPMENT

Glass measuring cup
Measuring cups and spoons
11-inch round baking pan
  or 13-by-9-inch pan
Large mixing bowl
Wooden spoon
Kitchen towel
Pastry brush

INGREDIENTS

1⅓ cups whole milk
¼ cup (½ stick) salted butter,
  cut into 4 even pieces
1 tablespoon granulated sugar
1½ teaspoons salt
1 teaspoon canola oil
4 cups all-purpose flour, plus
  more for kneading
2 packages (4½ teaspoons)
  active dry yeast
2 tablespoons melted salted
  butter, for brushing on top

1. **Warm the wet ingredients.**
In a glass measuring cup, combine the milk, butter, sugar, and salt. Heat in the microwave for 30 seconds. If the mixture feels warm like bathwater, stir it up. If it's not warm enough, heat it for 30 more seconds. Stir well. If the butter still hasn't melted, heat for 15 seconds longer, or until the butter is melted. (Be careful not to boil the milk or it will be too hot and the yeast will not bloom in the next step.) Grease the pan with the oil and set aside.

2. **Add the yeast.**
Put the flour in the mixing bowl and use your fingers to make a well in the middle. Pour half of the warm milk mixture into the well. Sprinkle the yeast on top. Using a wooden spoon, slowly stir the flour mixture while pouring the remaining milk mixture into the bowl. >>

TIP If you have a stand mixer, you can use it to knead the dough. Just use the dough hook in step 3 and knead until the dough pulls away from the sides of the bowl.

3. **Knead the dough.**
Sprinkle a handful of flour onto a clean work surface. Using the heel of your hand, press down on the dough, then fold the dough in half. Press down again, then fold. Keep kneading until the dough is soft and elastic, about 8 minutes.

4. **Let the dough rise.**
Pull the dough apart into 12 equal pieces. Using the palms of your hands, roll each piece into a ball. Arrange the dough balls side by side in the prepared pan. Cover the pan with a clean kitchen towel. Set aside in a warm spot in the kitchen to rest while the oven preheats, about 10 minutes.

5. **Preheat the oven to 400°F.**

6. **Bake.**
Transfer the pan to the preheated oven. Bake the rolls for 17 to 19 minutes, until golden brown on top.

7. **Let cool.**
Remove the pan from the oven. With a pastry brush, coat the tops of the rolls with melted butter. Let cool in the pan for 10 minutes, then serve. Although best eaten when freshly made, dinner rolls will keep in an airtight container at room temperature for up to 3 days.

PIZZA DOUGH

You'll be amazed at how easy it is to make your own pizza dough. Add any flavors you like—oregano, rosemary, Parmesan cheese—and experiment with the combinations you like best.

 NUT-FREE | MAKES ENOUGH FOR 2 MEDIUM PIZZAS | PREP TIME 1 HOUR 10 MINUTES

TOOLS/EQUIPMENT
Mixing bowls
Measuring cups and spoons
Whisk
Kitchen towel

INGREDIENTS
2 cups warm water (like bathwater)
2 (7-ounce) packages (4½ teaspoons) active dry yeast
2 teaspoons granulated sugar
¼ cup olive oil, plus more for drizzling
1 teaspoon garlic salt
4½ cups all-purpose flour, plus more for kneading

TIP Pizza dough will keep in an airtight container in the refrigerator for up to 1 week or in the freezer for up to 1 month.

1. **Bloom the yeast.**
Pour the warm water into a large mixing bowl. Stir in the yeast and sugar. Set aside until frothy, about 5 minutes.

2. **Add the remaining ingredients.**
Using a whisk, mix in the oil and salt. Add the flour, 1 cup at a time, stirring well after each addition.

3. **Let the dough rise.**
Coat a separate mixing bowl with olive oil and place the dough inside. Cover with a clean kitchen towel. Set aside somewhere warm until it doubles in size, about 1 hour.

4. **Knead the dough.**
Sprinkle a handful of flour onto a clean work surface and place the dough on top. Using your hands, knead the dough: Press down with the heel of your hand, then fold the dough in half. Press down again, then fold. Keep kneading until the dough is smooth, about 5 minutes. Shape the dough into a ball. It's now ready for you to roll out and cover in your favorite toppings. >>

HOW TO MAKE YOUR OWN PIZZA

When you make your own pizza, you get to control which toppings and exactly how much of your toppings to use. The possibilities are endless! Pro tip: Let your dough come to room temperature before rolling it out. It's much easier to stretch warm dough.

TOOLS/EQUIPMENT

Rolling pin
Pizza cutter or large knife

Pizza stone or parchment-lined baking sheet

INGREDIENTS

Pizza dough (the recipe on the previous page makes enough dough for 2 medium pizzas)
Marinara sauce

Cheese of your choice
Toppings of your choice
Olive oil, for brushing

1. Preheat the oven to 450°F.

2. Cover the dough with a kitchen towel and let it rest at room temperature while the oven heats up.

3. When the oven is hot, it's time to roll out the dough. Use a rolling pin to roll out half the dough (enough to make one medium pizza) to a circle that is about ¼ inch thick. Transfer it to a pizza stone or parchment-lined baking sheet. Cover with marinara sauce then add the cheese and any other toppings you like. Brush the exposed edges of the dough with olive oil.

4. Bake for 10 to 12 minutes, until the crust is browned and the cheese is melted and bubbling.

5. Let cool for 2 to 3 minutes before slicing and serving.

SOFT PRETZELS

A soft pretzel you've made yourself is the best kind of pretzel! Have plenty of melted butter or mustard on hand for dunking these beauties.

 NUT-FREE | MAKES 12 PRETZELS | PREP TIME 1 HOUR 30 MINUTES | BAKE TIME 8 MINUTES

TOOLS/EQUIPMENT
Measuring cups and spoons
Large mixing bowl
Rubber spatula
Large bowl
Kitchen towel
2 baking sheets
Parchment paper
Wooden spoon

INGREDIENTS
4 teaspoons active dry yeast
1 teaspoon granulated sugar, plus ½ cup
1¼ cups warm water (like bathwater), plus more for kneading
5 cups all-purpose flour, plus more for kneading
1½ teaspoons salt
1 tablespoon canola oil
4 cups hot water
½ cup baking soda
3 tablespoons coarse salt

1. **Proof the yeast.**
In a large measuring cup, combine the yeast and 1 teaspoon of sugar. Mix in the warm water. Set aside until frothy, about 10 minutes.

2. **Mix the dough.**
In the mixing bowl, combine 5 cups of flour, ½ cup of sugar, and the salt. Make a well in the center. Pour the yeast mixture into the well. Using a spatula, mix until a dough forms. If the mixture is too dry to make a ball, add 1 more tablespoon of water.

3. **Knead the dough.**
Sprinkle a handful of flour onto a clean work surface. Using your hands, knead the dough: Press down with the heel of your hand, then fold the dough in half. Press down again, then fold. Keep kneading for about 8 minutes. Shape the dough into a ball.

4. **Let the dough rise.**
Lightly oil the large bowl and place the dough inside. Cover with a clean kitchen towel. Set aside in a warm place until the dough doubles in size, about 1 hour. >>

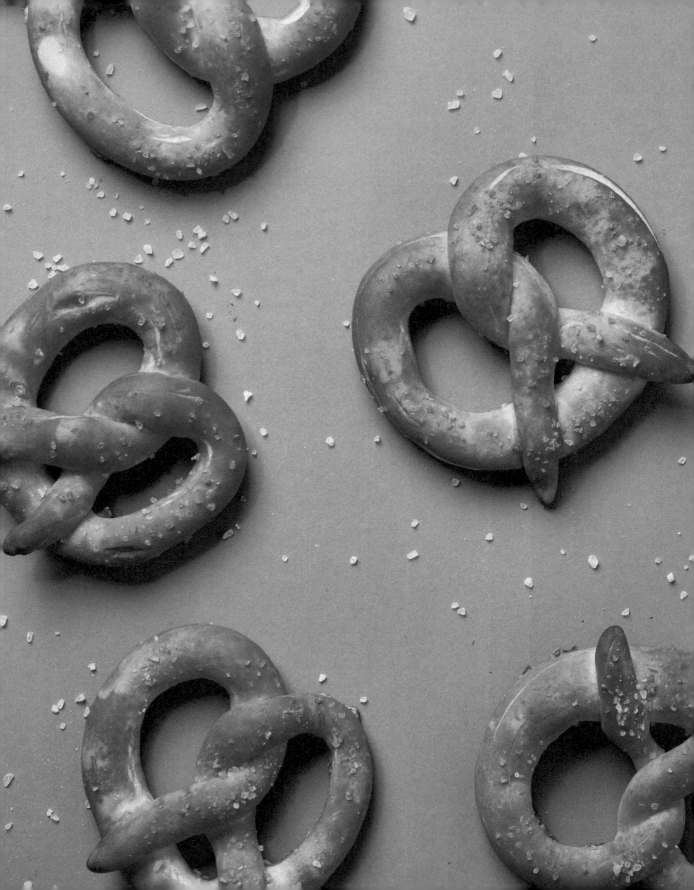

TIP Coarse salt has bigger grains than regular table salt. It's best for pretzels because it adds a nice crunch. Plus, it looks pretty and we always eat with our eyes first!

ASK AN ADULT to help you prepare the hot water bath, to dip the pretzels, and to rotate the pans in the hot oven.

5. **Preheat the oven to 450°F.**
Line the baking sheets with parchment paper.

6. **Prepare the hot water bath.**
Pour 4 cups of hot water into a large bowl. Add the baking soda and stir until dissolved. Set it aside to cool.

7. **Form the pretzels.**
Sprinkle another handful of flour onto your work surface. Place the dough on top and cut into 12 even pieces, like a pie. Using your hands, roll each piece of dough into a long rope. Form each rope into a pretzel shape. Dip each pretzel into the baking soda mixture. Place on the prepared baking sheets, spacing about 2 inches apart. Sprinkle with the coarse salt.

8. **Bake.**
Transfer the pans to the preheated oven. Bake the pretzels until brown, about 8 minutes. Switch the position of the pans halfway through (move the top pan to the bottom, and vice versa; also rotate the pans back to front).

9. **Let cool.**
Remove the pans from the oven. Let the pretzels cool on the pan for 10 minutes, then serve. Pretzels will keep in an airtight container at room temperature for up to 3 days.

SKILLET CORN BREAD

You can serve this cornbread with everything from chili to grilled chicken. Don't forget to leave some for breakfast the next day: Smothered in butter and honey, it's bliss on a plate.

 NUT-FREE | MAKES 1 SKILLET | PREP TIME 15 MINUTES | BAKE TIME 25 MINUTES

TOOLS/EQUIPMENT
9-inch skillet or pie pan
Mixing bowl
Measuring cups and spoons

INGREDIENTS
½ cup (1 stick) salted butter
1½ cups milk
1 large egg
1½ cups finely ground
   yellow cornmeal
½ cup all-purpose flour
½ cup granulated sugar
1½ teaspoons baking powder
1 teaspoon salt

1. **Preheat the oven to 425°F.**

2. **Melt the butter.**
Place the butter in the skillet then put the skillet in the oven to melt the butter. (This step makes the butter easy to mix and keeps the cornbread from sticking to the pan.)

3. **Mix the dough.**
Carefully remove the skillet from the oven and pour the melted butter into the mixing bowl. Set the skillet aside. Leave the oven on. To the bowl, add the milk, egg, cornmeal, flour, sugar, baking powder, and salt. Stir just until combined. Pour the cornmeal mixture into the hot skillet. >>

ASK AN ADULT to help move the hot skillet in and out of the oven.

4. **Bake.**

Transfer the skillet back to the hot oven. Bake the cornbread for 25 minutes, until a toothpick inserted into the center comes out clean.

5. **Let cool.**

Remove the pan from the oven and let cool before serving. Although best eaten within a day or so, corn bread will keep in an airtight container at room temperature for up to 3 days.

CHEDDAR AND BACON DROP BISCUITS

Full of Cheddar cheese and bacon, these easy drop biscuits are a taste of heaven.

 | NUT-FREE | MAKES 12 | PREP TIME 10 MINUTES | BAKE TIME 20 MINUTES

TOOLS/EQUIPMENT

Baking sheet
Parchment paper or silicone baking mat
Large mixing bowl
Measuring cups and spoons
Pastry blender or food processor
Ice cream scoop with thumb release

INGREDIENTS

6 tablespoons salted butter, cut into cubes
1½ cups all-purpose flour
2 teaspoons baking powder
2 teaspoons garlic powder
½ teaspoon salt
¾ cup buttermilk
2 cups shredded extra sharp Cheddar cheese
½ cup cooked bacon, crumbled

1. **Preheat the oven to 400°F.**
   Line the baking sheet with parchment paper or silicone mat.

2. **Work the butter into the dry ingredients.**
   In the mixing bowl, combine the butter, flour, baking powder, garlic powder, and salt. Using the pastry blender, work the butter into the flour mixture: Press down, twist, pull up. Repeat until the dough looks like small peas. (Alternatively, you can pulse in a food processor.)

3. **Add the flavor.**
   Add the buttermilk, cheese, and bacon to the dough mixture. Using your hands, mix just until everything is incorporated.

4. **Form the biscuits.**
   Using an ice cream scoop, drop mounds of dough onto the prepared baking sheet, spacing them about 2 inches apart. >>

5. **Bake.**

   Transfer the pan to the preheated oven. Bake the biscuits for 20 minutes, until the edges are slightly browned and a toothpick inserted into the center comes out clean.

6. **Serve warm.**

   Remove the pan from the oven. Let the biscuits cool on the pan for 10 minutes, then serve. Although best eaten when freshly made, these biscuits will keep in an airtight container at room temperature for up to 3 days (let cool completely before storing).

WHOLE-WHEAT CHEESE CRACKERS

Store-bought crackers don't stand a chance against these crispy, cheesy bites. Experiment with different flavors of cheese and salt to find your favorite combination.

 NUT-FREE | MAKES ABOUT 3 DOZEN CRACKERS | PREP TIME 40 MINUTES | BAKE TIME 15 MINUTES

TOOLS/EQUIPMENT

Large mixing bowl

Pastry blender or food processor

Mixing bowls

Rolling pin

Measuring cups and spoons

Baking sheet

Parchment paper or silicone baking mat

Butter knife or small cookie cutters

Wire rack

INGREDIENTS

2 cups shredded Cheddar cheese

1 cup whole-wheat flour, plus more for rolling

¼ cup wheat germ

1 teaspoon salt

6 tablespoons cold salted butter, cubed

3 tablespoons ice water

1. **Mix the ingredients.**
In the large bowl, combine the cheese, flour, wheat germ, salt, butter, and water. Using a pastry blender, cut in the butter: Push down, twist, lift up. Repeat until the mixture resembles small peas. (Alternatively, you can pulse in a food processor.)

2. **Chill the dough.**
Using your hands, shape the dough into a ball. Cover in plastic wrap and refrigerate for 20 minutes.

3. **Roll out the dough.**
Sprinkle a handful of flour onto a clean work surface and place the dough on top. Rub a little flour on the rolling pin, too. Roll out the dough until it's about ¼ inch thick.

4. **Preheat the oven to 400°F.**
Line the baking sheet with parchment paper or a silicone mat. ❯❯

ASK AN ADULT to help you cut the dough into squares or shapes.

5. **Cut out the crackers.**
   Using the butter knife, cut the dough into even squares, about 1 inch in size. (You can also use small cookie cutters to make any shape you like.)

6. **Bake.**
   Transfer the cut shapes to the prepared baking sheet. Bake for 12 to 15 minutes, until lightly browned and crispy.

7. **Let cool.**
   Remove the pan from the oven. Let the crackers cool on the pan for 5 minutes, then use a spatula to transfer to the wire rack to cool completely. Although best eaten when freshly made, cheese crackers will keep in an airtight container at room temperature for up to 3 days.

HONEY-MUSTARD PRETZELS

These pretzels are the perfect mix of sweet and spice.

 NUT-FREE · SERVES 10 · PREP TIME 10 MINUTES · BAKE TIME 1 HOUR

TOOLS/EQUIPMENT
Baking sheet
Parchment paper or silicone baking mat
Medium microwave-safe bowl
Whisk
Measuring cups and spoons

INGREDIENTS
¼ cup liquid honey
3 tablespoons Dijon mustard
½ teaspoon onion powder
¼ teaspoon garlic powder
2 teaspoons dry mustard powder
3 tablespoons salted butter, melted
8 cups mini pretzels

1. **Preheat the oven to 250°F.**
Line the baking sheet with parchment paper or a silicone mat.

2. **Prepare the butter mixture.**
In the medium bowl, whisk together the honey, mustard, onion powder, garlic powder, and dry mustard. Add in the melted butter and mix.

3. **Coat the pretzels.**
Spread the pretzels over the prepared baking sheet. Pour the butter mixture over the pretzels. Using your hands, mix the pretzels until evenly coated. Arrange the pretzels in an even layer.

4. **Bake.**
Transfer the pan to the preheated oven. Bake the pretzels for 1 hour, stirring every 15 minutes.

5. **Let cool.**
Remove the pan from the oven. Let the pretzels cool completely before serving. Although best eaten when freshly made, pretzels will keep in an airtight container at room temperature for up to 3 days.

GARLIC BREAD

So mouthwateringly soft and full of buttery garlic, you'll want to eat this bread with every meal.

 NUT-FREE   SERVES 6   PREP TIME 15 MINUTES   BAKE TIME 14 MINUTES

TOOLS/EQUIPMENT
Baking sheet
Parchment paper or silicone baking mat
Medium mixing bowl
Measuring cups and spoons
Bread knife

INGREDIENTS
1 loaf of French bread
6 tablespoons salted butter, very soft
1 tablespoon olive oil
4 tablespoons minced garlic
1 teaspoon garlic powder
1 teaspoon dried parsley

ASK AN ADULT to help slice the bread lengthwise down the middle as if you were making a giant sandwich.

1. **Preheat the oven to 400°F.**
   Line the baking sheet with parchment paper or a silicone mat.

2. **Slice the bread lengthwise.**
   Place the bread on the prepared baking sheet, cut-side up.

3. **Prepare the garlic butter.**
   In the medium bowl, combine the butter, oil, garlic, garlic powder, and parsley.

4. **Butter the bread.**
   Slather the cut side of each piece of bread with the garlic butter.

5. **Bake.**
   Transfer the pan to the preheated oven. Bake the bread for 10 to 14 minutes, until it's golden brown on the edges.

6. **Let cool.**
   Remove the pan from the oven. Let the bread cool on the pan for 2 or 3 minutes, then serve.

PULL-APART CHEESE BREAD

Ripping off gooey pieces of cheesy bread is fun and tasty. This is perfect party food.

 NUT-FREE | SERVES 6 | PREP TIME 20 MINUTES | BAKE TIME 20 MINUTES

TOOLS/EQUIPMENT
Baking sheet
Aluminum foil
Serrated knife
Measuring cups and spoons

INGREDIENTS
1 (16- to 20-ounce) round loaf of artisan bread
2 cups shredded Monterey Jack cheese
2 tablespoons cooked bacon, crumbled
¼ cup salted butter, melted

1. **Preheat the oven to 350°F.**
Line the baking sheet with aluminum foil.

2. **Cut the bread.**
Using a serrated knife, cut the bread into 1-inch strips in one direction, being careful not to cut all the way through the bottom of the loaf. Rotate the bread 90 degrees and cut in the other direction. You should end up with a cube pattern.

3. **Add the cheese.**
Tuck the cheese in between each row of bread. Repeat with the bacon.

4. **Add the butter.**
Transfer the loaf to the prepared baking sheet. Drizzle the melted butter over the bread. Fold up the ends of the aluminum foil and wrap the loaf tightly. >>

ASK AN ADULT to help you cut the bread.

5. **Bake.**

   Transfer the pan to the preheated oven. Bake for 20 minutes. Peel back the aluminum foil and bake for another 10 minutes, until the cheese has melted and the top looks golden.

6. **Serve warm.**

   Remove the pan from the oven. Let the bread cool on the pan for 2 to 3 minutes before serving.

BAKED TORTILLA CHIPS

For the best tortilla chips of all time, make these. Your favorite salsa is waiting . . .

 NUT-FREE | SERVES 10 | PREP TIME 10 MINUTES | BAKE TIME 12 MINUTES

TOOLS/EQUIPMENT

2 baking sheets
Parchment paper or silicone baking mats
Measuring cups and spoons
Small bowl
Whisk
Pastry brush
Knife

INGREDIENTS

2 tablespoons olive oil, plus more for the baking sheet
1 tablespoon fresh lime juice
15 yellow corn tortillas
Salt

1. **Preheat the oven to 375°F.**
Line the baking sheets with parchment paper or silicone mats. Brush the parchment with olive oil.

2. **Prepare the tortillas.**
In the small bowl, whisk together the oil and lime juice. Using the pastry brush, coat each tortilla with the oil mixture.

3. **Cut the tortillas.**
Arrange the tortillas in stacks of 5 or 6. Using a sharp knife, cut the tortillas in half, then in half again, repeating until you have 8 pieces. Repeat with the remaining stacks of tortillas. >>

ASK AN ADULT to help you cut the tortillas in step 3, and to rotate the pans in the hot oven.

4. **Bake.**
   Arrange the tortilla pieces in a single layer on the prepared baking sheets. Sprinkle with salt. Bake the chips for 8 to 12 minutes, until golden. Switch the position of the pans halfway through (move the top pan to the bottom, and vice versa; also rotate the pans back to front).

5. **Serve warm.**
   Remove the pan from the oven. Let the chips cool on the pan for 2 minutes, then serve. Although best eaten when freshly made, tortilla chips will keep in an airtight container at room temperature for up to 3 days (let cool completely before storing).

VEGGIE CALZONES

My kids love adding their initials with a fork to mark their own calzones.

 NUT-FREE | SERVES 4 | PREP TIME 20 MINUTES | BAKE TIME 10 MINUTES

TOOLS/EQUIPMENT
Baking sheet
Parchment paper or silicone baking mat
Measuring cups and spoons
Large skillet
Knife
Rolling pin
Fork

INGREDIENTS
1 batch Perfect Pizza Dough (page 157)
1 tablespoon olive oil
2 garlic cloves, minced
1½ cups mixed vegetables (e.g., matchstick carrots, frozen chopped spinach, diced bell peppers)
1 cup tomato sauce
½ teaspoon salt
¼ teaspoon black pepper
1 teaspoon dried oregano
All-purpose flour, for rolling
¾ cup shredded mozzarella cheese, shredded

1. **Make the pizza dough.**
   Follow the recipe on page 157.

2. **Preheat the oven to 400°F.**
   Line the baking sheet with parchment paper or a silicone mat.

3. **Sauté the vegetables.**
   In the skillet, over medium heat, heat the olive oil until it shimmers, about 2 minutes. Add the garlic and mixed vegetables. Cook, stirring, until the vegetables have softened, about 5 minutes.

4. **Add the sauce.**
   Stir in the tomato sauce, salt, pepper, and oregano. Simmer until the sauce has thickened slightly, about 5 minutes. Let cool while you prepare the dough.

5. **Roll out the dough.**
   Lightly sprinkle about 3 tablespoons of flour on a clean work surface. Place your dough on top of the flour. Slice the dough into 4 equal pieces. Use your hands, a rolling pin, or both to flatten each piece into a 12-inch round. ≫

ASK AN ADULT to help chop and sauté the veggies and also slice the dough into quarters, like a small pizza.

6. **Assemble the calzones.**
Add a generous scoop of the vegetable mixture to one half of each dough round. Top with cheese. Fold the dough over to cover the filling. It should look like a half moon. Using a fork, crimp the edges to seal. Pierce the top 3 to 4 times to let steam escape.

7. **Bake.**
Transfer the pan to the preheated oven. Bake for about 10 minutes, until the top is lightly browned.

8. **Serve.**
Remove the pan from the oven. Let the calzones cool on the pan for 5 minutes, then serve. (The filling will be quite hot.)

CINNAMON-SUGAR PITA CRISPS

Crispy and sweet, these pitas are the perfect afternoon snack.

 NUT-FREE SERVES 6 PREP TIME 15 MINUTES BAKE TIME 12 MINUTES

TOOLS/EQUIPMENT

Baking sheet

Parchment paper or silicone baking mat

2 small mixing bowls

Measuring spoons

Pastry brush

Wire rack

INGREDIENTS

6 whole-wheat pitas, cut into 6 wedges

3 tablespoons olive oil

2 teaspoons granulated sugar

1 teaspoon ground cinnamon

1. **Preheat the oven to 400°F.** Line the baking sheet with parchment paper or a silicone mat.

2. **Brush the pitas with oil.** Arrange the cut pitas in a single layer on the prepared baking sheet. Pour the oil into a small bowl. Using the pastry brush, lightly coat each piece of pita in oil.

3. **Top the pitas.** In another small bowl, combine the cinnamon and sugar. Sprinkle the the pitas with the cinnamon sugar.

4. **Flip and repeat.** Turn the pita pieces over and repeat steps 2 and 3.

5. **Bake.** Transfer the pan to the preheated oven. Bake the pitas for 12 minutes, until golden.

6. **Let cool.** Remove the pan from the oven and place the pan on a wire rack to cool. The pitas will crisp up as they cool. Although best eaten when freshly made, pita chips will keep in an airtight container at room temperature for up to 3 days.

CONVERSION TABLES

WEIGHT EQUIVALENTS

US STANDARD	METRIC (APPROXIMATE)
½ ounce	15 g
1 ounce	30 g
2 ounces	60 g
4 ounces	115 g
8 ounces	225 g
12 ounces	340 g
16 ounces or 1 pound	455 g

VOLUME EQUIVALENTS (LIQUID)

US STANDARD	US STANDARD (OUNCES)	METRIC (APPROXIMATE)
2 tablespoons	1 fl. oz.	30 mL
¼ cup	2 fl. oz.	60 mL
½ cup	4 fl. oz.	120 mL
1 cup	8 fl. oz.	240 mL
1½ cups	12 fl. oz.	355 mL
2 cups or 1 pint	16 fl. oz.	475 mL
4 cups or 1 quart	32 fl. oz.	1 L
1 gallon	128 fl. oz.	4 L

OVEN TEMPERATURES

FAHRENHEIT (F)	CELSIUS (C) (APPROXIMATE)
250°F	120°C
300°F	150°C
325°F	165°C
350°F	180°C
375°F	190°C
400°F	200°C
425°F	220°C
450°F	230°C

VOLUME EQUIVALENTS (DRY)

US STANDARD	METRIC (APPROXIMATE)
⅛ teaspoon	0.5 mL
¼ teaspoon	1 mL
½ teaspoon	2 mL
¾ teaspoon	4 mL
1 teaspoon	5 mL
1 tablespoon	15 mL
¼ cup	59 mL
⅓ cup	79 mL
½ cup	118 mL
⅔ cup	156 mL
¾ cup	177 mL
1 cup	235 mL
2 cups or 1 pint	475 mL
3 cups	700 mL
4 cups or 1 quart	1 L

DIFFICULTY INDEX

INDEX

ACKNOWLEDGMENTS

To my own mini foodies, Phoebe, Estelle, George, and Violet. Thank you for baking and tasting your way through this book. For being patient while I worked, and squealing with delight every time you got to help.

To Paul. Thank you for holding down the fort while I started a new career that turned into a whole new life. Your support has meant the world to me.

To my mom, who's always had so much faith in me, I've had no choice but to believe that I could do whatever I wanted.

To my friends who've encouraged me with compliments and cheers at every milestone.

To my mentor and idol, Margaret Roach, who shows me what success looks like every day.

To Clara Song Lee and Tracy Bordian, for transforming my ideas about "um, about half a cup of this" and "maybe a little of that" into gorgeous recipes even the littlest bakers can follow.

To Colleen, Barb, Jen, and Jill, for the pink mixer that started this whole dream.

ABOUT THE AUTHOR

Charity Curley Mathews is a former executive at HGTV.com and MarthaStewart.com, who's now a family food writer and speaker, contributor to Food Network, and founder of Foodlets.com, a website full of kid-tested recipes and ideas for teaching kids to love real food. She lives in North Carolina with her husband and four small kids on a tiny farm in the making, currently home to two naughty Lab rescues, eight chickens, two bunnies, and 100,000 bees.

2198231956808 9

CPSIA information can be obtained
at www.ICGtesting.com
Printed in the USA
BVHW051750131219
566460BV00001B/1

9 781641 523196